DROITWICH

NEVER
BROKEN

NEVER
BROKEN

My Journey from the Horrors of Iraq to the
Birth of My Miracle Baby

Hannah Campbell

with Sarah Arnold and Jill Main

JOHN BLAKE

Published by John Blake Publishing Ltd,
3 Bramber Court, 2 Bramber Road,
London W14 9PB, England

www.johnblakebooks.com

www.facebook.com/johnblakebooks ▪
twitter.com/jblakebooks ▪

This edition published in 2015

ISBN: 978 1 78418 424 7

British Library Cataloguing-in-Publication Data:

A catalogue record for this book is available from the British Library.

Design by www.envydesign.co.uk

Printed in Great Britain by CPI Group (UK) Ltd

1 3 5 7 9 10 8 6 4 2

Papers used by John Blake Publishing are natural, recyclable products
made from wood grown in sustainable forests. The manufacturing processes
conform to the environmental regulations of the country of origin.

Every attempt has been made to contact the relevant copyright-holders,
but some were unobtainable. We would be grateful if the
appropriate people could contact us.

To Mum, Dad, my brothers, Hamish, Josh and James, and my two daughters, Milly and Lexi-River: thank you for helping me become the woman I am today.

CONTENTS

CHAPTER ONE

THE BLAST

My first memory was of deafening silence. I was in a place somewhere between life and death when something primeval kicked in, making me use the last bit of strength I had to let out a guttural scream. Even if I tried my hardest to recreate it today, I don't think I'd be able to find that place inside me. I was screaming for my life, buried alive under tonnes of rubble in a sweltering coffin of dust after a mortar attack. If I wanted to get out of this, I just knew I had to scream and scream. The blistering forty-degree sun over the British military base, Camp Charlie, in the Iraq desert near Basra, had been blanked out by pitch-black darkness and there was a deathly quiet. I was entombed by hot earth and debris and every time I tried to open my mouth in an attempt to alert anyone I was still alive, I was choked by more dirt. It was packed so tightly against me that my nose was squashed and I couldn't even open my mouth properly. The pole that had pierced my face made it difficult for me to open my mouth

1

fully. I was so parched as the inside of my mouth, throat and even my eyes was coated with dust from the explosion. Mummified by wreckage so tightly packed, I couldn't even move my little finger. Each breath was a Herculean battle against the crushing debris that engulfed me. I was twenty-three years old, I had a two-year-old daughter Milly, and with every ounce of will I had inside me I knew it wasn't my time to die.

There's nothing comparable to the sense of abject horror and disbelief you feel when you regain consciousness and realise you are buried and you don't know if anyone will ever find, or even hear, you. When you suffer something so unspeakably terrible, I've been told your brain becomes incapable of storing the memories and it can even create false memories too. In many respects that's true. I lived my nightmare through a series of flashes – like glimpses of action through an old, flickering film reel. The darkness was not only due to me being buried five feet underground but also because my sight had been damaged. Both my eardrums had been perforated, so as sounds started to drift down to me they were muffled, gurgling and distorted, like I was under-water. A brain injury, caused by a piece of flying debris, left me semi-conscious with every one of my senses dulled. Despite that, on some level I knew I was trapped and I knew that my hands were pinned to my sides. That knowledge came not because I could feel them but because I became aware of my fingernails ripping off as I clawed in a futile attempt to free myself from what would otherwise become my dusty grave.

Ever since I'd been deployed in Iraq at the end of February 2007 I'd been terrified that I would be bombed when I was somewhere alone. I'd cried when rockets had whizzed over the top of my tent, night after night, fearing I'd fall to pieces if my worst nightmare happened to me. Now my fears had become my reality. Overcome with a strange, almost serene sense of calm, I didn't even feel any pain at first. When my blood began to run down my hands and my face from the pole that had unwittingly grazed my eye and impaled my cheek, I just registered that I was soaked with a sticky substance, with no comprehension that it was my own blood. The strangest part was that I felt like I had no legs at all. That sense of tranquillity, despite the horror I faced, then expanded exponentially until I had what I can only describe as an out-of-body experience. I felt like a ball of floating consciousness. There was no feeling and no pain, just a sense of drifting peacefully like nothing I'd ever experienced in my life. I honestly felt as though I was completely outside of my own body. It wasn't what I'd think of as a typical out-of-body experience as I didn't look down and see myself. In fact, I didn't see anything at all. It truly was like I'd become a bubble of thought. Perhaps it was my brain injury, perhaps I was still dazed or maybe it was my body's final act of self-preservation; I honestly can't explain what it was.

I later discovered your brain fills in massive blanks during trauma, so even now I can't be 100 per cent sure of what was real and what wasn't, but I'm convinced it did happen. I've also spoken to other soldiers at the military rehabilitation centre Headley Court in Surrey who have faced death. They have told me first-hand how they've experienced similar sensations.

Then, as if someone had clicked their fingers, I was back in my body and a steam train of reality hit me. Everything instantly became colourful and in focus, as though life itself had been taking place through a blurred camera lens and in slow motion.

I still didn't fully comprehend the horror of what was happening to me but I thought: 'Oh my God, you're going to die! If you let yourself drift again you'll never see your daughter Milly. If you want to hold her and see her grow up, you need to keep screaming.'

Pain hit me, like another wave of reality. It took me years to even acknowledge to anybody that I remember feeling such agony for I couldn't talk about it. I was afraid that if I let it in, because it was so terrible, that it might consume me again. It was the most exquisite pain ever: so horrific, so awful it would have been so easy to let it overwhelm me. I had to battle inside my own head to be able to scream over it. If I gave in, I knew I would have passed out and then I would have had no chance. I thought of the photo of Milly, which I carried in a pocket of my uniform next to my heart. Although I couldn't touch it, as my arms were pinned down, knowing it was there gave me comfort. I willed myself to believe that I would see her again. It was like thinking of a long-lost memory that I had a daughter who I couldn't give up. It was a massive mental battle, the biggest of my entire life, but somehow I managed to keep screaming.

The next thing I remember is hearing voices with American accents somewhere beyond the pitch-black darkness, along with a faint sound of digging. Members of the American Special Forces, who were in a neighbouring camp, had heard the explosion and come to help. It took them more than two and a half hours to dig me from the rubble; it felt like an eternity but in the Army you know the lads will do everything possible to get you out. So I had to stay alive and keep calling out to help them find me.

It seems ridiculous now, but hearing American voices triggered an idea of Hollywood action heroes in my mind and that planted a seed of hope. There was a weird little part of my brain that thought: 'God, it's the Americans! I'm actually going to be saved.' It wasn't to do with not having faith in the British Army, as my loyalties absolutely lay with them, but it was like an alternate reality and Hollywood films are where all the happy endings are, aren't they? That's how my brain was working. It was completely surreal. Then I could hear the clanking of spades getting closer and I think I heard my colleague, Lance Bombardier Karl Croft, shout: 'Hannah, we're coming! You need to hold on.'

There are no words that can describe the terror you feel – that you might die alone, in the ground, crushed by rubble and dirt. You just cling to the hope that they'll get to you before death does. Hearing Karl say: 'We know where you are, we can hear you' was the most comforting thing I've ever heard in my life. I told myself: 'Just hold on, they're coming', then suddenly there was light and I saw the silhouette of a grey military helmet, which is what the Americans wear. This was quickly followed by a sensation of being pulled. It was Karl, who was terribly injured himself, who pulled me free from the rubble. He was the man who saved my life that day. I must have been holding on for them because as they reached me, I had a massive heart attack and they fought and fought to bring me back. I vaguely remember being put into the back of a vehicle before darkness consumed me again. Exactly when it was I'm not sure, but the next flash of reality I have is of waking up in the field hospital in the most excruciating pain. A doctor was holding my hand up, trying to stem the blood loss from it, and I realised it was split in two, with the tendons showing inside, but I was too dazed and drugged to react. The fuzziness I'd experienced before had gone. It was replaced with a raw, brutal pain that made it hard for me to absorb anything that was going on around me.

I looked at the doctor and said: 'What's happened to me?'

'You've been hit in a mortar attack but we are helping you,' he replied.

Then the awful gravity of what had happened hit me like a tsunami. In reaction I shouted: '*No!*' That was the first time I realised I'd been badly hurt on some level before darkness engulfed me again.

The next time I regained consciousness was in the field hospital. Everything seemed chaotic, jumbled and confused as my mind wasn't functioning normally – I'd suffered a bleed on the brain from the debris that had smashed into me.

A doctor leaned over me, saying: 'Hannah, can you hear me? Hannah...'

I struggled to focus on him, amazed at what I could see over his shoulder. Alongside all the usual medical paraphernalia I experienced a bizarre hallucination where I could see hundreds of people like ants beavering away in the background. They seemed tiny, as if I was looking through a telescope backwards. I was somewhere reality and unreality seemed elastic; life itself hung in the balance. They must have knocked me out with a sedative as yet again I slipped into unconsciousness.

The next time I came round was as terrifying as being buried in the ground because the hospital was being bombarded in a mortar attack. I remember the mortar alarm went off and I became absolutely hysterical. Then there was a really close bang. I lay, unable to move, on a stretcher while the medical staff crouched down next to me. One doctor laid a normal set of body armour over me – it must have been the only thing they had to hand to protect me in case shrapnel flew through the room. Because of the urgency my injuries demanded, within seconds of each siren going off the doctors and nurses calmly carried on working on me again. In my confused state it was like the attack and my living horror was never-ending. When the threat finally passed over my sobbing from terror turned to tears of relief. I was just so grateful to the doctors and nurses for carrying on regardless. I owe them everything.

Despite the horrific reality of my situation, I realised someone else was going through exactly the same as me. I became aware there was a hospital trolley next to mine and in it was a male soldier being treated. Out of the corner of my eye I watched intently as he started fighting with the doctors and nurses – fighting everything that was going on and repeatedly trying to get off the bed. I think he was shouting as I could see his mouth was moving, but I couldn't hear anything. I just remember the violence of the situation, without fear, in my peripheral vision. I think that man was Karl but I can't be 100 per cent sure. Everything then went on fast forward around me – people rushing around, a dizzying chaos that left me spinning until it all went dark for hours again.

The job of the field hospital is to save your life and get you well enough to survive the flight back to Britain, where surgeons will then start the job of putting you back together. My family had been informed I'd been injured at midnight UK time, just three hours after the blast, and within minutes of me being found alive. Since then, they'd all sat waiting for an update phone call from the hospital, playing through all sorts of nightmarish scenarios in their minds. Already they'd been told I was seriously injured, but because of the nature of war it takes time for information to get through as the priority is saving your life. Also, what many people don't realise is that our wounds can take days to come to light since soldiers are often too ill to say where they hurt. So medics save your life, treat any other life-threatening injuries and get you stable. That means, since injuries are often so complex not every detail will be known. As they waited, my family was tortured by every fear imaginable: What if she's blind? What if she's severely brain-damaged? What if she's not the same person when she comes back? So although it was probably horrific hearing what was wrong with me, it was also a relief to hear I was alert and that I was still 'me', albeit desperately ill as my brain swelled and began to bleed from the impact of the injury. Not everyone was so lucky.

I woke up again at 4.30am and as I was more *compos mentis* my nurse helped me to take a few sips of water because I felt so parched. Then, in front of me, he rang my parents, followed by my husband, Jamie. He told Mum: 'Your daughter would like to speak to you.' I can't remember a thing about it as I was so drugged but apparently I said: 'I love you, Mum' and I was desperate to hear that she loved me too. Then I became very concerned about what had happened to my face – it was really hurting – and not much else. I told her, although it was garbled: 'I'm coming home. Will you meet me at the hospital?' Mum says she was reassured by hearing me say those words but she just wanted to hug me. Instead, she told me it was all going to be OK and she would see me there.

Then the phone was passed back to the Intensive Care nurse, who explained I would be flying back in around forty-eight hours once I was stabilised. I remember he started listing some of my initial injuries and telling Mum what was wrong: a pole through my face, a bleed on the brain, a smashed right hand, high-velocity shrapnel wounds to my hip and stomach, a completely shattered left leg that also had a pole through the thigh. They also told her that I'd had a heart attack as they pulled me free. I truly believe I'd had the heart attack in the rubble, before I was pulled clear, as that's when I felt I had left my body.

After speaking to Mum I drifted off to a more peaceful sleep. Sometime later I came around again, this time in a kind of dream-like state – except it was a nightmare. My brain had swelled so badly from the impact injury that reality remained distorted. The doctors and nurses who were treating me became, in my mind, strangers who were violating me. I didn't want them to touch me as I didn't understand how badly injured I was. I started swearing and shouting at them to get off me. I don't know if I fought them. Of course I had no nails left to claw at them but I've since been told that I did fight my imaginary enemy. Ultimately, I had to be sedated, as I was so traumatised I was fighting everything and everyone inside my own private nightmare.

My next flash of reality was waking up to see some medical staff looking over me. I kept trying to tell them I couldn't see properly and it frightened me, but I don't know if any words came out for they didn't seem to pick up what I was saying. At this point I became increasingly frustrated that no one seemed to understand. I also remember people kept asking me questions – 'Hannah, can you hear me?' 'Hannah, do you know where you are?' – but I couldn't see or hear properly to answer them and that made me even more confused. Because my brain was swollen and bruised, I suspect that what I thought were words were not what I was articulating. It's quite scary that what seems like a reality can actually be something quite different to what those around you are experiencing. I spent hours in this nightmarish state of hallucination, barely clinging to life.

My first true sense of coming back to reality came a day and a half after the blast, when I was still in the field hospital. By then I'd had two lots of emergency surgery to clean my shrapnel wounds and remove the poles that had pierced my body. My friend and camp roommate, Corporal Sally Allison, was sitting next to me and she smiled at me as I opened my eyes. Unfortunately, as she leaned over me to say hello, she knocked my catheter, which was full, and covered herself with wee. So, as I woke up, I started laughing, which broke the tension of the moment quite a bit. After she said hello, I reached up to touch the left side of my face as it was throbbing. To my dismay I realised countless stitches snaked up my cheek and past my eye, which they'd operated on as quickly as possible after the blast to minimise scarring. They had also stitched my hip and stomach up and my left leg was in an open half-cast as the swelling was so bad that surgery to try and save it at that time was impossible. I didn't particularly register my leg – all I wanted to do was to see my face.

'Sally, can you get me a mirror from somewhere?' I asked her.

She replied: 'Hannah, I don't think that's a good idea.'

But I'm stubborn and I insisted: 'Sally, I really need to see what's happened to me. I want to see what's happened to my face.'

After looking at one of the doctors, who nodded, she got

me a hand-held mirror. I remember just staring for ages in silence: I looked like a monster. A pole had pierced through my left cheek, leaving me with only 20 per cent vision in my eye. The impact of the rubble and stitches had left me swollen beyond recognition. I was so shocked, drugged and concussed that I stated quite matter-of-factly: 'I look like the Bride of Frankenstein.'

I didn't cry, but internally I was gutted. 'Oh, my God, is my face going to stay like this?' I thought. But I also felt a weird sense of relief for I had feared that maybe I'd dreamt it all. Looking in the mirror I could recognise that I hadn't gone mad, I wasn't trapped in some kind of hallucination or nightmare, something really had happened to me as I had the injuries that proved it to myself. The doctor came and told me that as soon as I was stable enough I was going to be flown back to the UK.

Later that day, he came to see me again and for the first time I asked him: 'What have I done to my leg?' I was aware there had been a lot of activity down there but I couldn't really feel any pain as they'd given me so many drugs.

I was shocked to the core when he said: 'Hannah, you really need to pay close attention to what I'm about to tell you: there is a chance that we might not be able to save your leg.'

I refused to acknowledge what he was saying to me. Recognising I was in denial, he gently repeated himself. At this I started shouting: 'No! No! *No!* I'm saving my leg. You've *got* to save my leg!'

There was no way I was going to lose it. He was lovely, listening to me, and I could see him clearly weighing up the options.

He then said: 'OK, Hannah, but if we don't amputate you

are going to fly back to the UK and you are going to have a major operation when you get back.'

And I said: 'OK, I'm willing to do that' and that was the end of the matter. I never thought about it again; I just thought I'd fly back to Britain and it would be fixed. In order to protect myself from the horror I refused to consider any alternative – I couldn't allow myself to comprehend the alternative: becoming a war amputee. If I allowed myself to think about it that made it real, so I refused to think about it or discuss it with anyone further.

In the hours before I flew home, I was well enough to look at my leg for the first time. I still had a leg and above the ankle was smooth, unmarked skin, but from just above the ankle down was a block of dark, purple swelling which was unrecognisable as a limb. What was once my foot looked like a breezeblock at the end of my leg; it was cut to pieces. They'd cleaned it up by the time I saw it, but still there was blood everywhere and it looked pretty horrendous. It was like I was wearing an ankle boot of disgustingness. Fascinated, I stared at it for ages, thinking: 'God, that's really malformed!' Even when I saw the shocking reality before my very eyes, I told myself: 'It's just an op. They can fix it.' Somehow I convinced myself it was a broken bone. 'I'll have six weeks in plaster, have a few plates, and then I'll get on with my life and forget about all this,' I told myself. It was at the time an act of self-preservation as I was still unable to comprehend the horror of what I'd gone through. It would take me years to do that.

As I lay in my hospital bed waiting to be wheeled out onto the tarmac to fly home, I thought the biggest irony of all was I shouldn't be there. I'd taken someone else's place: someone else's destiny. Just forty-eight hours before, one of my friends in Iraq, Corporal John Lewis, had asked if I would take over his shift as guard commander. Nobody wanted to do guard duty. It was an absolutely shit job and one of the most hated on camp. The main guardroom had no air conditioning, you got no sleep for the entire twenty-four-hour shift – unless you snatched an hour here and there on a mattress – and it was the worst duty you could get on camp, apart from cleaning the Portaloos. There was a huge amount of responsibility attached to it as you had to sign for all the live rounds, which were then issued to the guards. You then commanded those under you to 'load' and 'unload' at the start and end of the duty. Every single bullet that anybody had in their magazine or fired had to be accounted for and the buck stopped with you. Signing for one hundred rounds, any of which could have killed somebody, was a huge weight on my shoulders. If a bullet was lost, there had to be an investigation. Getting away for food and drink was also an issue and the twenty-four hour shift left you utterly exhausted. I hated the idea of it, but when John told me there was a chance he could get a flight a day early to be home with his kids I had no hesitation in volunteering to replace him.

'I'll do it if they give you a seat on an earlier plane,' I said. When a seat became available, I was delighted for him. 'Right, well, pack your bags, you lucky sod!' I told him. 'Your tour is over.'

He hugged me tightly as he was so excited. 'I owe you one,' he said.

'Don't be silly,' I replied. To me it wasn't a big deal as I was going to be stuck in Iraq anyway, but to him it meant leaving the shithole of Camp Charlie behind and getting back to his loved ones for good. He'd served his six months; he'd

13

done his time. He was fed up and he desperately wanted to go home and see his family and kids. I understood where he was coming from. My daughter Milly had celebrated her second birthday shortly before I was deployed, but during the two and a half months I'd served so far, I'd missed Mother's Day and I ached to see her and my husband, Jamie. The truth is, as a mum you deal with a lot of guilt for not being there for your child – you miss so many milestones, moments you can never get back. But then so do the dads.

Before leaving home I told myself that Milly was so young she wouldn't remember me not being there, but when I got out to Iraq and the realities of war had kicked in, and when I became wise to what war really was about, I felt regret for being so quick to leave her. Although I always knew the time away from her was going to be a big deal, what I hadn't factored in was that I could lose my life. Also, I hadn't taken into account the terror on a daily basis. I thought: 'If I don't get out of here I've robbed my daughter of a mum.' While I had immediate regrets, it could just as easily have been my husband Jamie in this position and then our daughter might have been robbed of a dad. The same can be said of any of the men and women who served alongside me, so there's no right answer. Mums and dads are equally important to their children yet we both have a role in our Armed Services. While there's been a big debate about it, both should be able to serve on the front line.

That's not to say they want to be there. No matter how rigorous your training, regardless of whether you are a mum or dad, a new recruit or veteran, it's virtually everyone's dream on long-term deployment to get back home and see your kids and family. I wanted to do everything I could to help John do that for I knew had it been the other way round somebody would have done the same for me.

Guard duty started at 6pm after I'd already done a full day's work. Staff had to meet at the guardroom and the shift ended at 6pm the next day. The Garrison Sergeant Major came, issued me the bullets, gave me a 'make sure you don't fuck up' briefing and then left me in charge.

I was really lucky as working alongside me as my second-in-command was Lance Bombardier Karl Croft, who was highly experienced. Originally, he was to have taken the Guard Commander role, as he was more senior than John. But as I wore a higher rank than both of them, the commander role transferred to me. That meant Karl became my second-in-command. Although I knew what I was doing, Karl was level-headed, experienced and a really nice guy, so he was great to have onboard. I also made sure everyone on duty was paired off, as guarding the periphery of camp could be a dangerous place. One of my deep-seated fears was to be stranded alone in the pitch-black of the furthest reaches of the base during a mortar attack and being blown up completely alone, with no one to hear or help me. I didn't want that to happen to them.

Just before we started the shift there was some gunfire in the distance. Sometimes shots were fired because there was a celebration in Basra, which you could see in the distance from Camp Charlie, but we couldn't be sure if it meant there were insurgents (rebel fighters against the new Iraqi government, who also targeted the coalition armies who were helping them) in the area, so we were immediately on heightened alert. Karl helped me organise who would be doing what: pairs in two-hour rotations throughout the night and following day, and each shift was written on a white board just inside the Portacabin where the guardroom was.

Briefing the lads, I told them: 'This is where you are supposed to be, and when you are supposed to be doing it. Don't fuck me around and don't fuck up. Apart from the first rotation, the rest of you can knock off for an hour, send your emails and make your calls and then come back.'

Family is everything when you are on tour. The reality is that while these lads do an amazing and courageous job, their families are their lifeline: they want to call their mums, speak to their wives and kids on the phone and pick up their emails or a parcel from home. Anybody who has served in a war zone knows and respects that, from the lowest to the most senior rank.

When the lads were dismissed I returned to the guardroom alone as we had what was known as an 'Occurrence Book'. I needed to record the distant gunfire so that the next team on duty would be aware of what had gone on and I also needed to make necessary radio checks. Once that was done, I briefly popped outside to have a cigarette with Karl, where we made chit-chat. I remember saying, 'I hope we're going to have a quiet night'. Then I walked back inside and in a split second my life changed for ever.

The building took a direct hit from a mortar bomb, obliterating it and leaving me alone and trapped underneath, but the next moments are a complete blank. For years I would get really frustrated as I wanted to fill in the gaps of what happened. I know there's no point in me straining to try anymore as I'm never going to get it back. Even today the only way I can comprehend what happened is through my injuries.

I left Iraq on an Aero Med plane, which is literally a flying hospital, exactly two days after the blast. All flights left Basra at night as the cover of darkness meant there was less risk of being attacked by a missile. I was pushed out onto the tarmac by a one-on-one nurse, who was to care for me all the way home, just like you'd get in an Intensive Care ward. Lying on my back due to my injuries, all I could see was the stars in the night sky. The air was warm and balmy, with just the sound of voices in the background as they prepared the flight.

Just before I boarded, my Garrison Sergeant Major came to see me: the highest non-commissioned officer in the camp. I was so off my face on painkillers, the only thing I slurred to him was: 'It's a really good job I had my bikini line waxed the night before I got blown up!' When the nurse told me this later, I was mortified. Apparently he took it well, although understandably he went slightly puce and muttered, 'Very good.'

As I was wheeled inside the plane I started crying, saying: 'What if they mortar us as I can't get off the stretcher?' 'My nurse said: 'No – you will be OK.' I felt such profound terror that they decided to sedate me. Halfway through the flight I stirred when the plane's engines seemed incredibly noisy. Military planes aren't insulated in the same way as commercial planes. I looked sideways and saw someone with plasters and bandages all over his legs and face: it was Karl Croft. He'd managed to come on as a walking casualty rather than on a stretcher. It was comforting to see him there, even if he did look a bit like an Egyptian mummy.

My nurse patted my hand and said: 'Go back to sleep. Everything's OK. We're on the way home.'

As I drifted off into a deep sleep, my thoughts turned to

being back home and with my family. My last memory before blacking out is of seeing Milly's smiling face in my mind's eye and an overwhelming feeling of relief I was heading home.

CHAPTER TWO

CHILDHOOD AND JOINING THE ARMY

As I blinked my eyes open several times the pain in my head was just excruciating. At first I struggled to focus, then I saw a bedside table with some flowers. The small picture of Milly I always carried under my body armour close to my heart was propped against the vase and, looking down at my body, I became aware I was wearing a hospital gown and tightly tucked into a bed. After a few seconds the reality set in: I was back in the UK and safe. A wave of relief washed over me.

A nurse seemed to come from nowhere. She took my hand and said: 'Hannah, you're in Intensive Care at Selly Oak Hospital in Birmingham. You're safe and we're going to make you better again. Squeeze my hand if you understand what I'm saying.' I used all my strength to give her hand a tight squeeze, she smiled at me and with that, I drifted back off into sleep.

This was the pattern for the next few days in there as I slowly began to recover. I was in a sort of half-state between waking and sleeping, mainly because of the painkillers I'd been given. The times I was awake soon began to increase and it's fair to say lying in bed gives you a lot of time for reflection. I was in a lot of pain with my injuries, but even then I had decided I needed to find the strength to fight back to good health: I had Milly and Jamie to think of, as well as my family, and I couldn't, and wouldn't, let them down. I found my memory drifting back in time to everything that had lead me to where I was that day.

It's fair to say that when I first joined the Army I was more Private Benjamin than a serious recruit. But what life in the Army gives you is a grit and backbone that will get you through anything in life and I knew this was what would help me battle back now. Even as a little girl I was made for a career in the Army, although I thought I wanted to be a pharmacist. With three brothers: Hamish, who is three years younger, and the twins, Josh and James, who were born five and a half years after me, it was a male-dominated household and I was very much a tomboy. Pride in those who served in the Military had been instilled in us as both my mum, Ann, and dad, Mac, had met in 1973 at RAF Leconfield, near Beverley in the East Riding of Yorkshire, where Dad was an aircraft technician and Mum was a dental nurse. Throughout my childhood I'd spend hours playing 'Armies' with the boys at the bottom of our garden at Bourne in Lincolnshire, before we later moved to a village in Cumbria. I'd chase my brothers and friends with plastic guns, rolling around in the mud. Holidays and after school were taken up with adventure games, which more often than not involved plastic guns. Mum and Dad bought me Barbie dolls but I wasn't interested and instead loved my Knight Rider pedal car.

Day-to-day, home life was very traditional but Mum loved the outdoors and weekends would be spent orienteering and walking in the countryside, although probably, with hindsight, my parents were desperately trying to tire out four boisterous kids! Dad had a way about him that now I've been in the Military I recognise. He never needed to shout at us and underneath he was a big softy and a fantastic father, but when he told you to do something you knew you had to do it. His was a quiet authority that didn't need a raised voice to make you act on it. Every weekend he would say: 'Right, go and tidy your room.' We'd all go and do it and then we'd wait and he would come up and inspect our efforts. The basis of it was personal discipline and taking care of your belongings but 'room inspection' is fundamental to Basic Training in the Army, so even as a child I was completing the first stages of my very own training.

Dad was also incredibly clever with his hands and he made us a go-kart he had fashioned from an old Silver Cross pram, powered by a two-stroke engine. We'd whiz around the local park and were the envy of the kids in our village. Then, one year, we had a flood in our home and the insurance company replaced all the downstairs floorboards and carpets. Dad used the wood to make the biggest treehouse you've ever seen, with all mod cons, including the old, ruined downstairs carpet, which he dried out. It was a good eight feet off the ground so I had to climb up to it from a long rope ladder and it was entirely carpeted.

My parents never pushed me to conform or become more

girly, instead encouraging me to be myself, so when I insisted on joining the Boy Scouts at fourteen years old, with two other girls, they supported me completely. My brothers were joining and when I found out all the brilliant things the Scouts did, I said, 'Well, I want to be a Scout, too.' I didn't see why girls couldn't do something which was so much fun, so I was accepted, along with two other girls from my village, as the first female Scouts in our troop. We kayaked in the Ardèche in France and went rock climbing; I even got a badge for tug-of-war. Back then, joining the Scouts as a girl was very unusual but even as a little girl, I was very much one of the boys and so when I joined the male-dominated environment of the Army I felt totally at home.

At sixteen I took a job working in Waterstones bookshop following my GCSEs. I wasn't a nine-to-five sort of girl, though, and I yearned for a more exciting life, beyond the isolated community in Cumbria where my family lived. Desperate to spread my wings, a career in the Armed Forces appealed as a way of seeing the world and getting paid for it too. My parents were delighted and really supportive as they'd had great careers in the forces and thought I had exactly the right temperament and personality to do well. Crucially, Britain hadn't been involved in any conflicts for years; Iraq and Afghanistan weren't major crisis spots and most people had no idea where they were. So, at the age of seventeen, I applied for all three Services. The first thing you have to do is a BARB Test, which is a psychometric test, but it also looks at your academic ability. This determines if you can join and what job you can do within the Army, RAF or Royal Navy. I passed the test for all three.

What swung it in the end were two booming, gruff corporals

at the Army Careers Office in Barrow-in-Furness. They made the Army sound amazing, just like my childhood camping and orienteering weekends with the Scouts. So just like that I giddily signed on – clueless as to the realities of Army life. The Careers Office held a weekly running club, which I joined to prepare myself for one of the key elements of fitness: running a mile and a half in under thirteen minutes. They'd shout gentle encouragement at us when we were running, and I thought: 'This is OK, I can handle this.' How different can Army life be? Little did I know! At the age of seventeen I swore my Oath of Allegiance at Barrow-in-Furness Army Careers Office. I read the words from a piece of paper with a small group of others who were also signing up. Serving my country wasn't on my mind until that moment, but when I stated the words, 'I will serve Queen and country' and it resonated with me deeply. I felt a real pride as I took the first major step into my new life.

Straight away I was technically in the Army, but I had a month to wait for my Basic Training to start so during that time I carried on with the running club. Now it was a different ball game completely as I was technically a new recruit; they started ordering me about a lot more and beasting me to make the timings on the runs. 'Oh, this is harsh!' I thought. Later, I realised they were getting me ready for what was coming next but the truth is, nothing prepares you for what you walk into when you start Basic Training in Winchester. Within minutes of being dropped off by my slightly tearful, yet proud parents, the other raw recruits and me were being yelled and shouted at like we'd never been before. I joined a group of terrified teenagers huddling together, scruffy as hell in our civvies and plastered with make-up. Straight away, we were thrown full-throttle into military training, aimed at making us physically and mentally tough. The privileges we had once enjoyed as a 'civvie' didn't apply anymore as we'd signed on the dotted line.

First, you are issued with your brand-new kit of everything you'll need during your Army career: three sets of uniform; a nuclear, biological, chemical suit; a helmet; two pair of boots; your sports kit, consisting of two pairs of shorts and two T-shirts; trainers; socks; a hold-all for carrying it in; a roll mat and sleeping bag; your rifle and webbing, which you carry your magazines in. It's all brand, spanking new and in packaging. Then you cart it through camp, which is like a Walk of Shame. Everyone knows you are the lowest of the low as the new recruits and all the while you are shouted at and firmly put in your place. The other soldiers make no bones about the fact they are in charge and you aren't fit to lick their boots. You aren't allowed to wear civvies. Instead, you either have to wear your Army camouflage gear or, if you aren't in uniform, the only thing you are permitted to put on is an unflattering tracksuit you are issued with: Ron Hill leggings and a green sweatshirt. A cardinal rule is that you're not allowed to wear your beret either, as you have to earn that; make-up is also banned. For the first week you are left reeling in shock.

I was in a mixed platoon, where boys slept on one floor and girls on another in rooms of six. Inevitably, where there's a bunch of teenagers there is flirting, but it was always very childlike, just like at school. Interpersonal relationships within the platoon were completely forbidden and during Basic Training nothing ever happened as we were all too scared, and to be honest, you were kept so busy with PT, block inspections, cleaning your kit and kit inspections or going to briefings and studying for tests that you were too tired for anything else, including sex. We weren't allowed off camp to go drinking so the only source of booze open to us was a Naafi-run bar. No one bought any alcohol – we knew PT the next morning would be so gruelling it wasn't worth risking a hangover.

For the first six weeks they break you down before building you back up again. We were never fast enough or tidy enough, and we didn't march well enough. The instructors teach you exactly how to iron a crease down the front of your trousers and razor-sharp creases down your sleeves too. I'd done my own ironing since the age of sixteen, but I still had to learn how to present my kit. You are taught to march, stand to attention, salute and how to clean your rifle, put it together and care for all your kit. One pair of boots would have to be polished for 'everyday' wear, but you do something called 'bulling' with the second pair, which is where you put on a thick layer of polish for a few days, then you apply water and cotton wool over days and days in a circular motion before repeating the process again and again to get them to the really high shine you see on the regimental parades. Once you pass out of Basic Training everybody cheats and buys lacquer and sprays them instead, but until then your boots have to be immaculate and done the hard way.

Then there's hours and hours of physical training to build you up for your first big test at the six-week mark: your first attempt at the Army Obstacle Course, which has elements of running, climbing, jumping, crawling and balancing with the aim of testing your speed and endurance. It's an absolutely punishing schedule as no one has the necessary strength or endurance to do it; you just have to dig deep and persevere.

But even though it was hell, I loved it. Week by week, kids dropped out when they found they couldn't hack it. I remember one got a knee injury and another just decided it wasn't for him, but for me that was never an option. I never rang home and said: 'Mum, please get me out of here!' – I never wanted to, and I just got on with it.

But while I toed the line with pretty much everything, I've always had a rebellious streak and during Basic Training there was one rule I just couldn't stick to, and that was not wearing any make-up. From the age of sixteen I'd never left the house without my 'face' on – brown eyeshadow, pink lipstick, foundation, black mascara and a peachy blusher. I wasn't vain but Mum had taught me always to make the best of myself and I liked to be groomed as it boosted my confidence. At home I wouldn't dream of going to the corner shop without lipstick, mascara and blusher on at the very least, so when we were ordered to have scrubbed, fresh faces it was never going to be something I could stick to. Every day I'd put on black mascara and a subtle sweep of peach blusher on my cheekbones and I seemed to get away with it for a while. When I got cocky in week three and tried to add some lip-gloss it was a step too far, though.

The instructor barked: 'Are you wearing make-up?' and ordered me to his office. He had a 'pull-ups' bar on the doorway and while he did his admin, he made me hang off it by my arms for ages. Each time I dropped off, he shouted at me to hang off it again until I was so physically exhausted I thought my arms would drop off and I couldn't do it any longer.

His one mistake was he didn't confiscate my contraband and even his punishment didn't deter me – I just stuck to the blusher and mascara and, apart from when I was deployed in Iraq, I never served a day in the Army without wearing at least some make-up. Of course, there were countless other occasions when someone barked: 'Private, do you have make-up on?' I'd say: 'No, Sir', then quickly go back, scrub my face and reduce the amount I had on, so I didn't get caught out again.

Army punishments are always memorable and everyone goes to extraordinary lengths to avoid them. One night we managed to get hold of some contraband clear-spray lacquer to buff our floor for a room inspection at 6am the following morning. We polished feverishly until 4am, trying to get it shiny like a pin. But while the floor passed muster, they smelt a rat so not much else did. First, some dust was found on some pipes and then a plughole wasn't sparkly enough. Each time they found something wrong the instructor bellowed: 'Ten times round the block! Get away! Get away! Get away!' and we'd have to run ten laps around camp before standing to attention in front of our beds again.

Then they moved to our lockers. You'd have beads of sweat as yours was inspected. At first, just like everyone else, I got the presentation of my kit wrong and so I spent a lot of time in stress positions – a favourite was holding yourself in a press-up position. Other times, if you'd been on exercise and you hadn't scrubbed your mess tins until they were sparkling like brand new you knew you'd spend the next few hours doing a ridiculous amount of sit-ups. My worst punishment was a hundred press-ups outside in the pouring rain as I had failed a locker inspection – my clothes hadn't been folded properly. An instructor stood next to me as I shouted out every single one in the downpour to make sure I completed it. Ultimately, it was all character-building stuff and I soon started to learn the 'tricks of the trade' to get through. For instance, in order to get the arms of my uniform completely flat and the creases razor-sharp, one of the girls showed me how to cheat: sneaking hairgrips up the sleeves of my shirts in the locker so it would sit perfectly.

Despite my efforts, unfortunately things didn't always go to plan. During another inspection limescale was spotted in the shower cubicle. I spent all day Saturday and Saturday night scraping it off the plugholes and ancient floor tiles and grout, which were clogged with years of grot. To complete the task I was unceremoniously handed a toothbrush and a bottle of bleach and told to scrub away, which was all very Private Benjamin! It was a grim and thankless task and I realise now, with hindsight, I was never going to get it spotlessly clean: it was the principle of making you work for it and ensuring you took pride in your kit and room.

One of the other 'tricks' I learnt was to never use the soap in your locker – that was your 'for show' soap. During locker inspections if you had used it they would find a micro bit of dust and oh, my God, if they found a body hair in your locker you were just annihilated! A positive effect of the punishments was that all the new recruits bonded over a shared hatred of the instructors. We also learnt that you were only as strong as your weakest link: if you were rubbish at something, not only did you get shouted at by the instructors, but as soon as they left the room, your platoon then shouted at you as well as everyone was dished out the punishment. That, in turn, made sure everyone pulled their weight, worked together as a team and had each other's backs. Ultimately, that's how I was able to cling on in the wreckage of the building after I'd been blown up, for I never doubted for a second that the lads, which is how we referred to both male and female recruits, would come for me.

At the six weeks' mark you were allowed to wear your beret for the first time, which was such a privilege. You also had to face the Army obstacle course, which everyone feared, as the punishment for failure within a set time would be severe. After weeks of PT, I was the fittest I'd been in my life and my final preparation consisted of a good night's sleep and an extra dash of waterproof mascara and a bit of lipstick to give me confidence. It started brilliantly. I tackled the three-foot wall, was given a leg-up over the six-foot wall, pulling myself up and over, walked the plank, rope swung over a muddy, watery ditch without falling in the murky water, and crawled on my hands and knees under a cargo net. It was incredibly tough but I kept up with the lads, partly due to the fact we were all getting screamed at by the officers to 'go harder and go faster'. Working as a tight-knit team, everyone encouraged those at the back to push themselves. One girl fell by the wayside, dislocating her kneecap halfway round, so they started rushing us over the rest of the obstacle course as quickly as possible.

Dripping with sweat, I remember facing the twelve-foot cargo net, which after my tree climbing as a kid was a doddle for me. When I scrambled to the top there were that many of us on there that someone swung their legs over the top, just as I was going over, and booted me so hard, they sent me flying off. I remember whizzing through the air before landing like a sack of spuds with a horrible thud. Then I lay there, feeling really winded and groaning in pain. A normal cargo net is supposed to be wider at the bottom so you will hit the net and roll down, but this one wasn't wide enough so instead of hitting the net I crashed into the ground. As the minutes passed, I still struggled to catch my breath and the pain of being winded didn't get any better. I realised that I must have injured myself. At this point I was put on a backboard by paramedics and taken by ambulance to hospital, where they discovered I'd fractured a vertebra in my back and fractured my sternum.

I was sent home from Basic Training on sick leave, which was gutting. I had to wear a big 'doughnut' neck brace and I couldn't return to Basic Training for six weeks. When I finally healed, I initially went into the rehabilitation unit to get me back to standard. There's a stigma surrounding being in the rehabilitation platoon in Basic Training. It's not the same as Headley Court, where men and women begin their often-heroic fight back from terrible injuries. Instead, in Basic Training the rehab unit is perceived as an easy life, where the worst you've faced is PT and the assault courses, not IEDs (Improvised Explosive Devices) and mortar attacks. Because of that, I knew I wanted to get out of there as quickly as possible so I passed all the fitness tests within three weeks. Then I was 'back-squadded', meaning I rejoined my Basic Training where I'd left off with a different platoon, who had just reached week six. That was the platoon I passed out with.

That incident on the cargo net was definitely a sign of things to come!

While being 'back-squadded' wasn't unusual, joining a new platoon was daunting. Yet, it led me to meet two people who taught me life-lessons that have shaped the person I've become. The first was another fresh-faced new recruit, Nikki Jarvis, who took me under her wing and who is the best friend I ever made in the Military. I ended up sharing a room with her and she immediately made me welcome and helped me settle in, introducing me to everyone.

At the six-week point you also go on the first of a series of all-night exercises, which is a real bonding experience with your platoon and culminates in an exercise called 'Final Fling' that you have to complete in order to pass out. Luckily, I was paired with Nikki, who shared my wicked sense of humour. We were taught to use Hexi-blocks, which are like large firelighters on which you cook your Army rations or boil-in-a-bag meals. You must also dig a hole for two people, then you have a piece of camouflage tent material called a 'Basher' and you must pin it up above your hole at a slight angle so any rain rolls off it; the two of you live in there during the exercise. You have a roll mat you put in the mud hole and you sleep on top of that in your sleeping bag. It was freezing cold and the weather was wet and miserable but we were like two naughty schoolgirls at a sleepover. During the exercise we had to change socks and powder our feet and there was a foot inspection to ensure everyone was looking after their health and had changed them. It's an essential part of Army life to look after yourself – you can't fight or work if your feet are in a mess.

The first night out also meant you'd be doing 'Stag'. This is another term for sentry duty. Hearing the dreaded words 'You're on Stag' on being woken in the dead of night minutes after you'd only just finally managed to drop off as it was freezing and uncomfortable isn't the most pleasant experience. There's also a practice enemy attack using bangers that produce smoke to make it as realistic as possible. I relished every moment of it and by the end of the exercise Nikki and I were firm friends.

Nikki had a way of making some of the worst experiences in training a laugh – and throughout our friendship when things got tough she'd be my panacea. The first time I saw it was when we had to test our gas mask in a room full of CS gas. We were down the queue and so we had to endure seeing everyone else come out with their eyes streaming, desperately trying to waft the gas off themselves. Then we both entered the room together with our masks on, walked round to stir all the CS gas up and then took them off and got a nice taste of it as we shouted out our name, rank and number. It was horrible! The first sensation was of burning in my nostrils and eyes, then tears poured down my face so hard I couldn't see. Nikki dragged me outside and laughed at me crying at how awful it was, while coughing, gagging and spluttering until I was in stitches, too.

We also learned to fire a gun together for the first time in our lives. You are initially taught on an electronic range and then you complete a weapons handling test: how to prepare to fire, make it safe, load and unload. Following this you are issued with a gun with live rounds. Part of passing Basic Training is passing your range test – hitting targets at different distances from a variety of firing positions during the day and night. The fundamental rule is to always keep your weapon facing down the firing range and never at someone else. The first time I ever fired a live round I thought: 'Oh, my God, if I fuck up here I could actually kill someone!' It felt like a real weight of responsibility, having a live round in my rifle, and we weren't just firing blanks. Everyone feels like that at first and it's vital never to lose that. It was very much at the forefront of my mind that one day I could be firing at a person, yet if it was a choice between my life and someone who was going to kill me I wouldn't have hesitated. You always need to justify to yourself that if you were to take a life then you've done so for the right reason.

As well as the hard work, during the second half of Basic Training there are chances to have the odd night out. One evening in particular cemented my bond with Nikki. We joined some of the lads on a night out in Portsmouth, which was notorious for trouble between Navy and Army personnel and the locals. I don't know why, unless it was the fact we were with a group of lads, but without any warning, when Nikki went to dance, a civilian girl came up behind her and smashed a glass bottle over her head. She fell to the floor, somehow managing to land a Frank Bruno-esque right hook on the girl's nose as she went down. Immediately, I ran over and joined in to stop her getting a kicking.

Unfortunately, after landing a few punches and pulling the girl to the floor by her hair, we were both unceremoniously kicked out of the club by the bouncers and then the police were called. I was terrified. Getting caught fighting in the Army is the worst thing ever – you can end up not only getting charged under civilian law, but also being charged under military law, so it was a massive deal. On top of that, I was even more terrified my parents would find out. Luckily, the police believed us when we told them what had happened and after a stern ticking-off, they drove us back to camp without telling our Commanding Officer or the Military Police. It did earn us kudos with the other Army girls once word got out, though, so after that no one wanted to mess with us. And the truth is, even though I'm ashamed of being involved in a cat-fight, at the same time I wouldn't have left my best mate in trouble and taking a beating. You don't want to ever mess with the Military as they always look after their own. Since then Nikki has repaid my favour in spades.

The second person who had a massive impact on my younger self was an instructor, with whom I had a torrid fling during Training. It's a fundamental rule that trainee soldiers and instructors do not have interpersonal relations. Being caught risked a strict punishment or at worst, a Court Marshall. But after I was 'back-squadded' I had new instructors and there was an instant chemistry between one of them and me. I've always been incredibly shy when it comes to men and I wear my heart on my sleeve, but he showered me with attention at an age when I had never experienced anything like it before. The painful truth is, I was like a lamb to the slaughter and it was actually quite pitiful with hindsight. Six foot four, he was dark, broad, achingly masculine and extremely good-looking – and he knew it.

Funnily enough, if I met a Lothario like him now as thirty-year-old me, I wouldn't go for him. But at seventeen, a cocky, sure-footed guy taking an interest in me made him all the more attractive. My only other relationship had been with my childhood sweetheart, who I'd met at school. We'd both been shy, innocent and fumbling teenagers from the age of fifteen to when I joined the Army, so a worldly man in his late twenties seemed incredibly sophisticated.

Right from the outset he made it very clear he wanted me, and he made his move at the earliest opportunity, when we were allowed to leave the barracks for the first time for a group meal, two months into Basic Training. We were only permitted two pints each but they went straight to my head after months without an alcoholic drink. After chatting me up, we shared a surreptitious kiss and the excitement was added to by the fact it had to be clandestine. Then he invited me back to his room, saying: 'Would you like another drink?' and I nervously agreed. After sneaking across the parade square to his quarters I ended up snogging the face off him. It was intoxicating and it would have been so easy to let myself be seduced, but I said: 'No, I'm not happy to take things further yet.' He was used to having young recruits as putty in his hands so he seemed taken aback that I wasn't willing to sleep with him there and then, but I was adamant and I left, creeping back across the parade ground to sleep alone in my bed. From there it was a really slow-burner. He'd steal me away for a kiss whenever he could and he charmed me, taking me out for dinner several times a week and buying me small gifts.

It was an exciting and heady courtship and to me the whole star-crossed lovers' thing seemed incredibly romantic. For him, with hindsight, it was all about the thrill of the chase. After a few weeks he suggested taking a weekend's leave at the same time. I stayed with a friend and he came and stayed in a nearby hotel, taking me out every night and wining and dining me while remaining the perfect gentleman. Though I still kept him at arm's-length, I was falling head over heels for him. I was genuinely flattered and it was the first time in my life I had been treated like a lady and wooed. Back on camp, at every opportunity he would whisk me away for a snog. Even when we were getting our final measurements taken for our dress uniform for the passing-out parade he called me to his office for a clandestine kiss and a cuddle under the pretence of getting my belt for my uniform.

Straight after my passing-out parade, instead of going home with my parents who had come down to watch, I went to

London with a group from my platoon to consummate our relationship. Because the instructors get leave at the end of every passing out, he came to join me and we stayed in a luxury hotel. That night was memorable for what it was, as he taught me what sex without love could be. Although I thought I was in love with him, it wasn't until I met my husband Jamie that I discovered how special that was. But for the first time in my life I knew what it was to desire a man and to be desired and charmed. A big part of the attraction was also the danger of dating a fickle charmer – he was like a kite on a blustery day. I also thought I was different and I could change him.

We stayed together for almost a year, spending every weekend together. But within months our relationship became fraught. At first, I had no reason to be suspicious. My parents have been happily married for forty years and my only other boyfriend was my school sweetheart. Yet, as soon as each band of new blood came in every twelve weeks, people began to stir the pot and say he was up to no good and he'd been seen with this or that new recruit.

In the end, perhaps predictably, he did break my heart. I found him out, having a relationship with a girl from another platoon, as a mutual friend had seen a sexy text he'd sent her confirming they were having an affair and she told me. When I confronted him, at least he was man enough to instantly admit it, saying: 'Yes, that's what I'm doing.' I was terribly hurt at the time but I got over him. He taught me two very valuable lessons – if a man really likes you he'll be prepared to wait. Second, never give up on love – you'll find it again, even if your heart has been broken.

After I completed my Basic Training I decided to initially train as a nurse in Gosport at the Royal Hospital Haslar and the University of Portsmouth. I thought it would be a way of using the skills I'd learnt and I would also learn some new skills, which I could use to help people, but literally from about day one I absolutely hated every second of it. I take my hat off to all the nurses who have helped me through the years as they have been instrumental in helping to save my life, but I just wasn't cut out for it at all. I didn't like the smell of the wards or the sight of blood that much. How ironic this is now, considering how much time I've spent both in wards and looking at my own blood!

The light-bulb moment happened quickly that as I'd loved soldiering in Basic Training I should be in a trade where you still had the opportunity to do that, so I transferred into the Adjutant General's Corps and an admin role. After being attached to an Infantry Unit, you then go and do your admin job but you do all the soldiering they do as well. This was the best of both worlds, I felt. My Phase Two training involved returning to Winchester for twelve weeks to learn a trade. I learned finance, the computer systems and accounting. Incredibly, Nikki from my Basic Training was also based at Winchester, so we struck up our friendship again where we'd left off.

Then, towards the end of my Phase Two training, I was sat watching TV when Nikki came in to see me. She was upset and clearly in shock. 'Hannah, please can I speak to you in confidence?' she said. 'I've got to tell someone what's been happening as I don't know what to do.' I made her a cup of tea and she admitted she'd just discovered she was pregnant after splitting from her boyfriend and she faced the prospect of becoming a single mum. It was a hugely emotional time for her as she'd had a scan and the medical staff hadn't let her see the images of her unborn baby because she hadn't decided what she was going to do.

Immediately I told her: 'You should keep your baby as you will always regret it otherwise.' She was worried she'd lose her Army career but I told her: 'You'll be fine. There's no reason why you can't still have a career in the Army as a mum. You can do everything if you really want to.'

Just days later I joined 47 Regiment Royal Artillery at Thorney Island, near Portsmouth, and lost touch with Nikki. I didn't know what her final decision was; I just hoped whatever she had chosen was the right choice for her.

My first 'real' job in the Army was a world away from the horror of Iraq. I started at the Regimental Headquarters as an office junior initially for three months. It was a grindingly boring job, which primarily involved being the tea girl and photocopying and filing for the Commanding Officer, Adjutant and the Regimental Sergeant Major until they checked you had a head on your shoulders. Only when they knew you wouldn't fuck up, did they let you loose and you were able to move on to more interesting work. One of the only perks was that for the first time in my Army career I was allowed to get my nails done – provided it was a natural-looking French manicure!

From there, in late 2003, I moved on to being an administrative clerk, overseeing the paperwork of around 200 soldiers, which is a better class of office job. Even though I didn't know it at the time this was a promotion that would lead me straight into the path of the man with whom I would fall in love and who would become my future husband.

CHAPTER THREE

JAMIE

It certainly wasn't the most orthodox or romantic of settings in which to lock eyes with the man who was to become your husband. Even now, the irony of my initial meeting with Corporal Jamie Campbell isn't lost on either of us. Incredibly, I was posing as a blood- and mud-splattered amputee after volunteering to play a casualty in a re-enactment of injuries for people doing their battlefield First Aid training course.

My task, throughout the day, was to portray someone whose arm had been blown up. I lay in a field, splattered in mud, in the pouring rain with a little tube that came up the side of me with a squirter for fake blood. The trainees had to practise putting a tourniquet on my 'injured' arm and I had to then squirt the blood over them in order to make it as realistic as possible. I was far from looking my best and it was hardly a sexy scene or conducive to romance.

Jamie was one of the instructors that day. Later I found out that he'd joined up in 1994 so he'd already served eight years in the Army. But I didn't look twice at him – I was too busy mucking about, playing the invalid. After my experience with the charming instructor, I didn't want to have my heart broken again, or get a reputation in the Army, as I'd never been that kind of girl. So men, other than having a laugh as one of the lads, were strictly off-limits for me.

At the end of the day everyone who took part went out for drinks. When I nipped to the toilet, I came back and Jamie was chatting to my friend, who introduced him to me. There was no denying he was handsome, self-effacing, a proud Scot and a really kind person and it was his personality that won me over. So, when a few of us decided to go back for a block party in my room, I asked him to join us.

Earlier that week I'd been learning to cannulate – where you put a needle in someone's arm for a drip – and we'd 'borrowed' some cannulas to practise at home. In my drunken state I said: 'Do you mind if I have a go on you?' And he said: 'Yeah, alright.' I ended up taking the blood from his arm. It sounds weird but it was such an intimate act that I knew there was definitely a vibe going on between us, but I held back as there was no way anything else was going to happen. Jamie was the perfect gentleman – not only did he let me butcher him with an extremely long needle without complaint, he didn't try it on with me at all. We just had a brilliant time and a laugh.

At the end of the night when he went to leave, I drunkenly gave him my mobile number and said to him: 'Text me!' and he did, the day after and then every day after that. It was just daft stuff and funny comments about how his day had been; at that time it was nothing romantic. I knew I liked him and I could tell he felt the same but I was determined not to rush into something again. Although I loved spending time with him we only met in a group for I was determined that we were only going to be friends at that point.

Jamie was ten years older than me and I'd been single since my disastrous fling so I wasn't particularly bothered about meeting anyone, and particularly someone in the Army. So when he asked me out, slightly nervously, a few weeks later, I said: 'I don't think I want a boyfriend at the moment.' He seemed a bit disappointed, but I shrugged it off. To some people, dating can seem like the best way to get over a broken heart but I didn't want to rush headlong into another relationship. Army life was much more relaxed and there was a massive social life – much like being students at university – so I was having fun and I didn't want to be tied down.

Every night we'd be out somewhere and Jamie would inevitably end up joining us, which meant I was able to get to know him without any pressure. Even after I initially told him no, there was no awkwardness between us as he was just a lovely man and a great laugh. Based at Pirbright Barracks as an instructor, every evening he'd ride his motorbike the 60 miles to Gosport to come and see me. As weeks turned into months he made his feelings for me clear by the way he touched my arm and the attention he gave me, but he was never pushy. As we spent more and more time together, with our friends, I started to have feelings for him. Our mutual friends started ribbing us, saying: 'When are you two going to get together?' 'Have you got together yet?' and even 'Have you sorted it out?'

Everyone was asking us and seemed to know it was going to happen. I'd dismiss it, saying: 'Don't be silly,' as I didn't want to act on the spark developing between us. One night he had a few too many drinks and so I said he could sleep in my room, in my sleeping bag. From then on, whenever we went out, he slept on my floor and then later he shared my single bed, yet still nothing happened between us. He'd come out with my friends, we'd have a laugh but later he'd just cuddle me, we'd talk and we'd go to sleep with his alarm set for 5am the next morning to give him time to ride to work.

He was so lovely and considerate that as time went by I fell completely head over heels for him and I knew Jamie was the man I wanted to be with. We went out for dinner and I said: 'I know you've asked me out quite a few times, and my answer is "yes". I love spending time with you.' There was no going back from that moment. That night Jamie kissed me for the first time and it was incredible. My whole body tingled and I had a funny feeling in the pit of my stomach. That night we became lovers and it was like nothing I'd experienced before. I think being truly in love with someone is one of the most amazing things in the world. It was much deeper and more meaningful than I'd ever known. Things couldn't get any better, I thought.

Jamie was the first man I ever truly loved. I started making plans for him to meet Mum and Dad and we even talked about going on holiday to France. All our friends said: 'Finally, you've got it together! What took you so long?'

But three months into our relationship my bubble burst when I discovered that he wasn't single after all. He'd left his phone on my bed while he had a shower and a text message flashed up on the screen from one of his mates, saying: 'Have you told her yet?' When he came back in the room I said to him: 'Jamie, you've got this message. What have you got to tell me?' His face went ashen and then he dropped a bombshell.

He said: 'I didn't want you to find out this way but I've got a wife and two kids. We are separated and we're not in a relationship anymore. I didn't tell you as I knew it would put you off seeing me.'

I stormed out of the room, completely devastated, and I felt so let down again. Distraught, I phoned my mum and told her the awful truth, confessing: 'Mum, I love him. What am I going to do?' She was surprisingly sanguine about the whole situation, saying: 'As long as you are sure he's separated and he's telling the truth and provided you truly believe he is serious about you, then you've got to decide if you really like him. If you do really love him and you want to be with him then you've got to accept his history as that's part of who he is. Being with him means you have to accept his children, so the next step is to ask him to meet them.'

So I took my mum's advice and I went back to my room where he was waiting and I sat on my bed and I said: 'If we're to make any sort of go of this there can't be any more secrets. There's no doubt I'd be happy to accept your children, but if you want to be with me you can't be married to someone else.'

Two weeks later I met Jamie's children. I was really nervous, but his son Craig, who was then six years old, and his eight-year-old daughter Laura were both lovely and after I introduced myself, I took them to a local park and I just talked to them. Over time I told them I really liked their dad and I'd like to be a part of their lives too.

Jamie proposed to me at the start of the summer of 2004 as soon as his divorce came through, nine months after we first met. He'd already rung my dad to ask his permission. There wasn't a big 'Will you marry me?' grand gesture. Instead, he was driving in the car somewhere and he said out of the blue: 'Shall we get married?' I just said: 'Yes, yes, of course I'll marry you.' In that moment I just knew it was right and that I wanted to be with him. He couldn't afford to get me the ring he wanted to get me, so two days after he proposed we went to our local jewellers and together we chose a gold ring with a single cubic zirconia. It was modest, but it didn't matter and Jamie promised that he'd replace it, when we could afford to do so, with a diamond ring.

I was just nineteen, and while some people may think I was young, I knew it was right. Both of us had to write letters to our Commanding Officers asking for permission to marry. It's a courtesy and tradition that is followed to this day. After permission was given, including a two-week holiday for our honeymoon, I couldn't wait to be Jamie's wife.

Organising a big white wedding and keeping everyone happy was a bigger headache than I thought. At nineteen years old I had a romantic ideal of love and everything started to get on top of me as we made lists of guests, who would be sitting where, where the venue would be, what we'd eat for the wedding breakfast, what canapés we should have, what dress I would wear, all the stuff that I just didn't want to do. So I eloped. I rang Mum and said: 'I've decided to just go and do it.' At first she was taken aback, particularly as she and Dad had put down a huge amount of money for our reception at a local hotel. But she called me back and said: 'Hannah, at the end of the day just do what makes you happy.'

Jamie just wanted to get married, so I booked in at the Register Office and got the next available slot the following month. On the morning of my wedding, on 30 June 2003, I didn't even have a dress. I ran to a wedding shop in town, managed to grab an off-the-peg plain white silk dress that I liked that was in my size and a matching shawl, then I spotted a pretty gold tiara and I bought them all. Then, I went into a nearby florist and lied: I said was getting married, my florist had let me down and could she make me a bouquet on the spot? She dropped everything and made me a loose bouquet of long-stem roses. Finally, I went into Debenhams department store and managed to persuade one of the girls on the Chanel cosmetic counter to do my make-up for free. Then I got dressed and turned up at the Register Office, where we were married with two of our closest friends: Private Becky Lovick, who I'd met during Basic Training, and Corporal Nick Manning, who had served alongside Jamie for twelve years, as our witnesses. I've never been one to follow convention and for me it was the perfect wedding.

Afterwards, I rang my parents and said: 'I've done it, I'm married!' On the one hand, Mum was happy that I was happy but, understandably, deep down I know they were both gutted not to have seen their only daughter walk down the aisle on her wedding day. Back then I didn't feel bad as I was in love and I was now Mrs Campbell and it was spontaneous and romantic. If I want something I'm very determined and I make sure I get it and the truth is we were deliriously happy.

Even now I look at my wedding pictures, taken as we walked out of the Register Office, and it makes me smile as we had big, beaming grins on our faces. Jamie had worn his Regimental Kilt and he looked so handsome and you can see how in love we were. At that point we didn't really care what anyone else thought, we just were wrapped up in each other.

Afterwards we headed to a local brasserie, where we had the most expensive champagne on the menu and toasted our new life together. We didn't ring Jamie's parents as we decided to drive to Scotland and so we turned up at their door, announcing; 'We've got married!' They were surprised we'd gone ahead before our planned big day but they were still delighted. Our wedding night was spent at a local hotel in the countryside. We were given a four-poster and they put rose petals on the bed and a bottle of champagne and chocolates.

Our two-week honeymoon was spent moving into a semi-detached Army married quarters in Thorney Island, which was our first home together. It was totally bare, with two bedrooms, standard Army-issue magnolia paint throughout, a blue bathroom and a green carpet. Although it wasn't the stuff dreams were made of, it represented us starting a life together, so we loved it. At first we sat on beanbags with two second-hand mugs, toasting our new life together with a pot of tea because as newly-weds we didn't have any money and we had no furniture. Mum and Dad soon forgave my impetuousness and they bought us sofas for our wedding present, which was the first bits of furniture we ever owned together. Mum then gave us old plates, and Jamie's mum gave us loads of her old furniture: a coffee table, chairs and a dining room suite and wardrobes as she was moving to a smaller house. We also laid laminate flooring over the carpet in the sitting room and painted it a cheerful yellow. The final touch was buying a barbecue so we could have our friends round in the evenings. So we had everything we needed.

Jamie and I were deeply in love at the beginning. We still loved each other at the end, but it was just in a different way. Throughout our marriage he treated me like a princess – he was so kind, probably too lovely. I was always strong-willed and I thought I was the tougher one of the two of us, while he just wanted to love and cherish me.

Within three months of getting married I decided I wanted a baby. 'Jamie, how would you feel about becoming a dad again?' I asked him. I said I could stop taking contraception and we could just see what happened. He was very laid-back about it and he said: 'Yes, if it happens, it happens.' I'd always known I wanted a family. I knew we'd be good parents – we were happy together, and we were financially secure so it was the next natural step to take.

It may seem strange, as I'd only recently been promoted to Lance Corporal, but I believed I could handle being an Army mum. In fact, I thought the world was my oyster and that with a baby I'd have a career and a family; I'd have it all. I fell pregnant with Milly shortly before we celebrated our first wedding anniversary. When I missed my period I bought a pregnancy test and I waited until Jamie came home to try it. When it came up positive we were overjoyed. Jamie hugged me and his tears welled up and he just kept saying: 'I can't believe we're going to have a baby!' Then I rang Mum and I told her: 'You're going to be a granny!' She was thrilled, then she asked me if I was going to give up work and I said: 'No way! There's a great nursery and I love the Army. I definitely want to be a working mum.'

The next day I went in to work and told my Commanding Officer, who said congratulations, and life continued pretty much as normal. Jamie took the afternoon off to come to my first scan at three months and it was incredibly emotional seeing for the first time a little peanut on the screen and a heartbeat and knowing it was our baby. I remember he said: 'It's so amazing we are going to have a little boy or a little girl of our own', and I couldn't wait for us to have a family.

Being pregnant in the Army was hard work, but I was looked after and supported and then something amazing happened, which was a huge help. I was told a new Private was joining my office and as soon as she walked in, I couldn't believe it. It was Private Nikki Jarvis, my friend from Basic Training. The minute we were alone she gave me the biggest smile and hug ever and said: 'I couldn't believe it when I found out I'd be working with you.' Then she pulled out a photo from her pocket of her daughter Chloe, who was six months old. She had tears in her eyes as she told me: 'I decided to keep her. Thank you for your advice. It was the best decision I have ever made in my life.'

For me it was an incredible moment to see that not only had she made the right decision, but she was also making it work as an Army mum. Being pregnant with Milly I'd felt a bit scared that my career wouldn't work out. Now I had the reassurance that if Nikki could do it as a single mum, I could do so too. So I told her I too was now pregnant. She immediately congratulated me and gave me another massive hug – it felt like fate had put her back in my path as from that day on, as an Army mum and Army mum-to-be, we were inseparable. We sat gossiping every day instead of doing our work. It didn't matter how rough I was feeling, I turned up for work every single day – even when I had the most horrific morning sickness. More often than not, Nikki would say: 'You don't have to do that, I'll cover that duty for you.'

There were a few occasions when I was really bad and when my boss, the Sergeant Major, saw me, he said: 'Go and get your head down for a couple of hours and if you feel up to it, come back.' More often than not, if I was ill Nikki covered and without her I'd have really struggled. As well as helping me at work she advised me on what cream to buy to avoid stretch marks, gave me some of her baby clothes and even felt my baby kick in my tummy in the office before Jamie did. I'd cover for her when she was off having her nails done and she'd do the same for me when I nipped out for fifteen minutes to get my eyelashes tinted by one of the mums on camp who was a beautician. We were always up to something, whether it was dodging work or trying to get out of being the tea girls. When we got sick of our boss asking for cup after cup of tea every day, we even tried squirting washing-up liquid in his tea. Instead of making his own he said our tea tasted so bad, we needed practice and he'd ask us to make even more cups for him.

There were only two big changes once I announced I was pregnant and apart from that my work continued as before. The first was that I didn't have to do obstacle courses anymore and I only did the PT that I wanted to do. Secondly, because I didn't get big enough to require a maternity uniform, I was allowed to wear no belt and my shirt un-tucked to cover my little bump. No one was ever negative: if anything, people wanted to look after me more as I was a mum-to-be and almost every rough, tough soldier I knew asked to see my baby scan when I came back to work after having it done.

But I always wanted to pull my weight. Two days before I gave birth I was lugging boxes of paper up and down stairs in the stock room as I was young and fit and it didn't occur to me this wasn't what everybody did. It was my first pregnancy and other female soldiers who were pregnant just got on with it. No one was forcing me to lug the boxes up and down the stairs – I did it because I wasn't ill, I was pregnant.

I breezed through the whole thing, with no problems or complications until I went into labour on 3 April 2005 – dead on my due date. It began early in the morning and after driving me to the maternity ward, Jamie held my hand throughout, encouraging me when the contractions got stronger and more frequent. But when I got to 10cm dilated, Milly's heart rate dropped and she went into distress. Immediately, the midwives and doctors went into overdrive and I ended up being rushed in to have an emergency caesarean (C-section) to save her life. Jamie was brilliant and he was my rock all the way through, supporting me and keeping me calm.

As I was still laid up in the operating theatre, as soon as Milly was born at 9pm they placed her in the crook of my arm. Initially she cried noisily, but as soon as I put her against my heart she just looked up at me peacefully. I felt such a massive surge of love and Jamie was so elated he started crying with relief. After she was handed to him, he cuddled her and he started singing her a Scottish lullaby. He was allowed to stay until 11pm, but then he had to leave me on the maternity ward. The next morning he was back at the crack of dawn and he said: 'I haven't slept a wink as I couldn't believe it.'

Although Milly wasn't Jamie's first child, he still made the experience incredibly special for me. I felt like I had it all. As soon as she heard I'd had a caesarean, Nikki was round, helping out all the time. Along with Mum she helped me with my washing, ironing and housework until I recovered. I got three months paid maternity leave followed by statutory maternity pay, so as soon as I was well enough to get out and about, Nikki introduced me to the Army wives. There was a great social and support network between them and you could always pop in to see someone for coffee, some advice or just a chat. For me, it was nice to meet the other halves behind the men.

The Army wives are the unsung heroes in many ways. They are the ones who stay behind and hold everything together. Army life would grind to a halt without them. It wasn't until I had Milly that I truly appreciated how essential they are. Their husbands disappear for six months at a time, they have three or four kids, yet they are the glue that holds everything together. And when the husbands come back, they might not be quite the same as the men who left, especially if it's been traumatic, and yet their wives support them and pick up the pieces. It's not easy being married to the Army. I was so grateful when they really welcomed me for it's an extraordinary support network.

Back at home, Jamie and I had to find our feet as new parents and right from the start, he wanted to be a hands-on dad. Even when I was on maternity leave he said that he didn't want to miss out so we made a little agreement that he would get home from work, play with Milly for an hour before bath-time and then put her to bed. While he was doing that, I would cook tea. That was his way of balancing things out. He showed me how to do nappies as he'd been there before, and when I was exhausted after being up all night when Milly was ill or teething, he'd tell me to stay in bed and he'd do the feed. Jamie also loved taking her out. He has always been a keen photographer and they'd travel all over the place to go and get photos of a landscape in the middle of nowhere.

I had a lovely six months off before returning full throttle to Army life, but this time with a little one in tow. From day one I had to be on PT Parade at 7.10am after dropping Milly off at nursery. PT usually involved a run or a Tab, which is marching at speed, carrying weights. So to juggle our work and baby commitments Nikki and I worked out a rota. Without Nikki, I don't think I'd have survived being an Army mum. Whoever wasn't on duty would go and pick the kids up from nursery in the evening. Jamie often worked away but when he was at home he'd also do his share. Between the three of us we managed to keep all the plates spinning most of the time and a few months after coming back, I was promoted to Corporal.

Part of returning to work involved 'Remedial PT' at lunchtimes: the gym or circuit training, which was never easy. Again, Nikki was still completing hers after her baby, so I had someone to go with. I struggled after the baby to get back to full fitness because of my caesarean and it was specifically aimed at people like me. It wasn't the usual 'beasting' – it was aimed at building you back up. There was also a weight-loss clinic, which helped me shed the baby weight, and within seven months I'd snapped back into shape and I was as fit as I was before.

As Nikki lived up the road from me in the barracks we were always in and out of each other's quarters so our girls grew up like sisters. On the odd days where she or I had been kept up all night with a sick or teething baby we'd cover while one of us had a lie-in, saying: 'She's just gone sick to the Medical Centre', knowing full well the other was probably still in bed. We weren't an unusual case in the junior ranks. Everyone covers for one another – it's drummed into you in Basic Training to work as a team. But as fellow mums, we definitely had a special bond. If one of us ran out of nappies, Calpol or just needed to let off some steam, then I was there for Nikki and she was there for me.

Before going to war I didn't think that anything would change despite being a serving mum. I didn't even consider not returning to work – I liked the idea of my daughter having a role model of a mum who worked and was independent. I also liked being a mum in the Army as I'd got to know the Army wives as much as their husbands so I had the privileges of both sides of the world. It didn't occur to me ever to leave after having her and I managed to balance it – I didn't always get things perfect but I did the best I could, even though it wasn't always easy.

One night we were told we would be called up for a training parade at 5.30am to see how fast we could get our kit together if we needed to. We had no idea when it was going to happen, just that it was something that could happen at any time, so because I had Milly to factor into the equation, I forward planned. I always had my kit ready to go in a bag by my bed just in case of an early roll call. It was sod's law, of course, that Jamie was away and he couldn't help me get out of the door. So I threw on my kit – my T-shirt was inside out under my Camo jacket but I knew no one would notice that.

Then I realised: 'Shit, what am I going to do with Milly? Well, there's no other option, Nursery doesn't open for hours, and I can't put her on one of the other mums at this ungodly hour of the morning, so she'll just have to come to the parade ground with me,' I thought. So I dressed her in her warmest romper suit and gloves, and grabbed the car chair that we kept by the front door. The whole point was to make sure we could react quickly and so I ran out of the door. I'll never forget the CO's face when I marched up, bold as brass with Milly in her baby seat in one arm, and saluted with my other arm, although he was clearly secretly quite impressed as I was one of the first arrivals. Then Nikki quick-marched down, carrying her kit and baby Chloe in a car chair too. Luckily, neither of the girls started screaming so we popped them down side by side together at the edge of the parade ground with a toy to keep them occupied. Then we did the inspection and when we were dismissed, we picked up our babies, went home, had showers ready for work and then dropped our daughters off at nursery as normal and carried on with our day's work. My saving grace was that Milly was a good-natured baby. If she'd been bad through the night, I don't know what I would have done! I still got the odd sleepless night but as it was my first baby I didn't know any different. Jamie was also a hands-on dad. He never shied from changing a nappy in the middle of the night or doing his bit when she wanted a feed.

For the first year after Milly was born, being a new mum I was protected from deployment abroad. Jamie wasn't, so at the time I just kept my fingers crossed he wouldn't be sent away. By the time Milly was two, soldiers had started to frequently go on six-month tours of Iraq and Afghanistan. Saddam Hussein had been overthrown and, memorably, I'd watched on TV as his statue was toppled from Firdaus Square in downtown Baghdad in spring 2003. At the same time, Afghanistan had a declining security situation and growing insurgency and NATO had agreed to take a leadership role in providing security in and around Kabul.

Slowly but surely, British regiments were being deployed and I knew that sooner or later it would impact on us and that one of us would be called up for a tour. It's funny, but neither of us wanted to talk about the inevitable, so we just carried on with family life. I was doing all my training exercises and so I knew either Jamie or I would be deployed. It must have been playing on Jamie's mind as one night he said: 'What shall we do if one of us is called up?' 'We'll deal with it when it happens,' I replied. I just couldn't face the thought of it so I didn't want to have the chat, but internally I was dreading the inevitable – that one or both of us would be deployed.

CHAPTER FOUR

GOING
TO WAR

Privately, I always hoped and prayed we wouldn't be called up for deployment in Iraq or Afghanistan. It was like an unspoken conversation between Jamie and myself that I hoped to God we would never have to face. Sadly, that wasn't to be. On 10 February 2007, Jamie was called in by his Commanding Officer and told that he would be deployed to Afghanistan with his regiment and given the dates. In an awful twist of fate, later that week, I was called by my Commanding Officer and told I had been selected to deploy to Iraq. Because we were parents the Army wanted to ensure one of us would stay at home with Milly, who was still only two years old, so it became a decision as to who would stay behind and who would go. My CO said: 'Go home, have a chat with your husband and decide what you want to do and come back to me with your plan tomorrow.'

That night, Jamie and I sat down over a cup of tea and

hammered it out. He said: 'My whole regiment is deploying to Afghanistan so it makes sense for me to go and for you to stay with Milly.' But I wasn't having any of it. I said: 'Well, I've been picked up on a trawl and I think I should go to Iraq as there's less risk out there and Milly needs her daddy as she grows up.'

A trawl is where individuals who have certain skills that are required in the theatre of war are chosen for deployment. This meant instead of going with 47 Regiment, whom I was attached to, I would go by myself and I'd be attached to another regiment once I arrived. Jamie was ten years older than me and I felt he'd already done his time as he'd served in Northern Ireland when the troubles were really bad, as well as Kosovo. He was also ex-Infantry and he had a lot of weapons skills so I felt that if he deployed then he might not be used in his current role, as an admin clerk, but that he would probably be used for other things. We both knew things were tough in Afghanistan. Rumours had spread like wildfire that his old unit, The Argyles, had had to use their bayonets for the first time in twenty-five years, something unheard of in modern warfare. I was terrified that if he went then he would end up being injured or worse.

We were both acutely aware there had been tragic loss of life in both Afghanistan and Iraq, but I felt the right thing was for me to go. My view was that even though I was a mum going to a war zone, it was no different from the hundreds of young dads going out to do their job and serve their country. Some dads are deployed when their wives and girlfriends are pregnant and the women give birth when they are away. They normally get compassionate leave for two weeks to meet their newborn baby.

As a woman, if I was pregnant I would never be deployed, but now I'd had my six months' maternity leave, returned to work, got back to fitness and it was time to do the job I'd signed up to do. Naively, I was convinced there was much less chance of me getting injured in Iraq, so even though I was desperately torn about leaving Milly, I felt it was the right thing to do for my family and ultimately this was the job I'd signed up for. When I gave birth to Milly and decided to stay in the Army I'd known that one day I might have to leave her and that day had come.

So the decision was made. I'm very single-minded and headstrong and I said: 'No, I'll go instead of you as it makes far more sense.' If I'm honest, Jamie didn't have much of a choice about it really as I steamrollered him into agreeing. I knew he would have liked to have gone as he's a proud man and it was hard for him to see his platoon go off and not be with them, but this was something I wasn't going to budge on. I did it for him and, in my mind, so our child would have a father. Ironically, at that time I believed Afghanistan, where Jamie would have been deployed to, to be far more dangerous than Iraq.

Once the decision was made Jamie did everything he possibly could to support me, just as he always did. I had only two and a half weeks to sort my life out and then go to my first conflict zone. My parents were absolutely devastated when I told them that night. Mum said she couldn't understand why I was doing it and asked if I'd really considered how hard it was going to be to leave my baby.

For me, preparations were so fast that I didn't really have any time to think about the consequences. I went to see Nikki, who was gutted that I was going but promised to help Jamie look after Milly while I was away and said that she'd support him for me.

Within days I kissed goodbye to Milly for the first time as I was placed as a priority case on an OPTAG (operational training and advisory group) course, where they had a town set up in ex-Army quarters. There were people dressed up as locals, playing the enemy; I had refresher training to teach me how to deal with the enemy, the rules of engagement the British Army follow, as well as methods used for clearing buildings and compounds. You don't just go storming into a building as there could be anyone in there, so I was taught how to check that it is empty and how to deal with the enemy if they are hiding inside, including warning: 'Stop or I'll shoot' before firing a round. You all have your weapon and everyone has to practise and re-practise through role-play. We were shown how to use equipment we might be given in theatre, given presentations on IEDs, showing what they could look like, what to expect and how to deal with them, how to recognise heat exhaustion in people, and there was even a talk on sexually transmitted diseases and protecting yourself over there. It was a pretty intense four days, starting at seven in the morning and ending at seven in the evening.

Every morning before it started I'd ring Jamie and tell Milly I loved her down the phone. I missed her terribly but I knew this was just the start and six long months in the Iraq desert stretched ahead of me. The British Army training is second to none but the fact is nothing can prepare you for the harsh reality of war. Everyone has to do the course, no matter what trade or rank you are.

Life seemed to hurtle towards deployment day and I wrote a will, took out life insurance and wrote a letter that says:

'Not to be opened until my funeral'. I still have it now and it's still sealed. In it, I planned my own funeral and I asked for Leonard Cohen's version of 'Hallelujah' to be sung. I also told Mum, Dad, Jamie and my brothers that I didn't want them to waste their lives grieving for me but instead to channel all their energies into looking after Milly. They weren't to wear black; instead I wanted them to celebrate my life and be proud of what I'd achieved. I also wanted Milly to have my medals when she was old enough.

Everything was efficient and practical and perhaps I was a bit in denial about the realities I faced ahead of me. As Jamie had eight years more experience than me in the Army he helped me pack my kit as he'd done in his Infantry days. 'Don't worry about Milly, I'm going to take care of her,' he told me. He recognised that that was one of the most important things and he helped me to choose lots of pictures of Milly to take so a bit of home would always be with me.

I also had my eyelashes tinted, my armpits, legs and bikini line waxed and my hair dyed – there are no beauty salons on camp. It's also impossible to wear make-up when it's so hot as it just slides off your face. A contraceptive injection was also booked in at the doctors – not for birth control, but so that I wouldn't have any periods. Every female soldier I knew did that when they were on deployment as it's one less thing to have to worry about.

One of the more difficult preparations was that your kit had to be marked with a number, made up of the first three letters of your surname and the last three numbers of your military number. You have to write it on the front of all your kit and body armour so that you are identifiable if you are injured or killed. It's not a nice thing to do at all. Jamie helped me write on the letters, but as we did it we were both silent, thinking about why we were doing it.

My parents came down a few days before I left. Mum tried to talk to me again about why I was doing this. I told her: 'Mum, I can't talk about this now. I just need your support while I'm there. I'm going to a war zone and I need to know you are there for me.'

Because I was going to miss Milly's birthday and Easter we had an Easter cake and she got to stay up really late. I put on a smile and made a pretence of eating, but inwardly I felt sick with nerves and I had no appetite. When we finally put her to bed I kissed her goodbye and told her I loved her and that I'd be home soon. In my mind I was already counting down the days until I'd be home again and I consoled myself she was too young to understand what Mummy was doing.

It was still pitch black at 4am the following morning when a dark green Land Rover came to pick me up from the door to take me to RAF Brize Norton. My best friend's fiancé knew how upset I was about going so he volunteered to do it to give me moral support. I said goodbye to Mum and Dad and to Jamie but I didn't cry – if I'm really honest, I felt numb. It's like when you wait for a holiday, and you are travelling to the airport and it doesn't feel real as you have been waiting so long for it. Jamie wanted to hold me and his last words were: 'I love you, Hannah.'

Anxious, I didn't speak on the two-hour drive. We stopped and got a McDonald's breakfast on the way, the last one I'd be able to eat for a while. Driving into the base I felt a knot of nerves twist inside me before I was picked up in a whirlwind of checking in, showing ID and going through all the protocols you have to do to ensure you've got all the kit you need with you before boarding a huge RAF aircraft with one piece of hand luggage. The most important item in my carry-on bag was a photo of Milly smiling in a pink romper suit.

On board, the aeroplane was just like a charter flight inside with seats. It's anything but a holiday experience, though, as you are all in kit and there's an air of expectation. It's not a pleasant feeling – you can sense everyone's trepidation about what they are flying into. Surrounded by other military personnel there was plenty of banter, but I didn't have anybody to share my jangling nerves with as I was flying as the sole member of my unit.

Before landing at our final destination in Basra there was a brief stop-off at Kuwait at a military airport. The Kuwait camp was a vast sea of tents. It was the middle of the night, the air was cool but there were unfamiliar sounds, and a silence fell on everyone as we waited to board the second plane. This time it was net seating for the two-hour flight and we had to put on full body armour. The lights were on as we left Kuwait but when we got to half an hour before landing, they were turned off – the mortar threat was very real. I looked around and all I could see was the whites of all of the lads' eyes in the pitch black. Fear was palpable as everyone was nervous about landing safely.

As we touched down at Basra Airport our nerves were justified as we suffered a mortar and rocket attack, which was quite a welcome. You couldn't see out to spot the telltale streaks across the sky, so the first we heard was the deafening crash of an explosion, which shook the plane. We disembarked with mortars still flying over our heads and they were strangely beautiful as they traced across the sky like shooting stars.

To be honest, at first I had no idea what was going on.

Then an alarm went off that sounded like a World War II siren you hear in the movies and we were all ordered to lie on the ground. For the second time that night all you could see was the whites of everyone's eyes, except they were wider this time in the moonlight. Seconds later there was another series of booms. We'd been travelling for twenty-four hours and were absolutely shattered; we all lay, quietly praying for the all-clear. Someone tried to break the tension by saying: 'Welcome to Iraq!' but everyone was rattled. Little did I know it but compared to the rest of my time in Iraq, the explosions I heard then were distant ones.

When it finally ended we were all ushered, shaken, into the airport to collect our bags. The staff, who were accustomed to regular onslaughts as a part of camp life, were all very matter-of-fact as they were used to the mortar alarm, but I didn't even have time to fully register what had just happened and its implications as I was so exhausted. There was a speech about a form we then all had to fill in that checks you into Theatre.

After I had collected my bag, I was greeted by the guy whose job I would be taking over. He led me through the camp, which was as huge as a small town. First, he took me to where I would be sleeping – a shack that resembled a large Anderson Shelter with individual rooms inside. On the mud floor you had some matting and a cot onto which you put your sleeping bag. You were given a laundry sack with a tag with your name and number on it. It was incredibly dusty from the desert everywhere, including the room, and it was stiflingly hot. To try and make it a tiny bit homely I placed a photo of Milly and Jamie above my bed and then managed an hour and a half's fitful sleep before I had to get up to be briefed about my new job.

My eyes were rolling in my head with tiredness as he explained my role was 'OPLOC' or 'Operational Location', a largely administrative role that involved checking people in and out of Theatre and briefing new arrivals. This could include full units arriving to individual people like myself coming in. A darker side of the job was checking who had been killed or injured. I started work later that day after a few more hours of getting my head down.

Although my job was initially admin, we were still acutely aware of the risks. The mortar bomb siren became almost a daily part of our lives. The second we heard the warning, dropping to the floor became an automatic reaction. The abnormal becomes the grinding norm and we lived on our nerves, constantly aware of the threat. Just as terrifying was the fact that kidnap and rape became risks. The reason the kidnap threat was stepped up was that someone had stolen some of the camp laundry. The system in place was that you'd stick all your dirty kit into the sack you were given, which was tagged with your name, dump it in a huge laundry bin, they'd take it away and twenty-four hours later, you'd collect it from another bin. Somehow some uniforms had gone missing.

I can only speculate, but I suspect it would probably have been local guys who were threatened that their families would be killed if they didn't do it. But it meant there was a risk (albeit a relatively small one) that someone might try to enter the camp or trick a patrol. The reality was they probably wouldn't have got very far as they'd have been stopped at the gate and all patrols were aware of the risk – and no one was taking any chances.

What I hadn't expected about camp life was that it wasn't totally self-contained and insular. Every day locals would turn up at one of the gates to be employed in various roles inside the camp as contractors. Some hated what you stood for, and particularly as a woman, as pretty much every adult female we saw from outside wore a hijab or a burka. We weren't allowed to walk around in groups of less than four because of the perceived risk, so it meant that if you wanted to go anywhere on camp you had to have someone with you. You were also warned there was a risk of snipers and that one had shot at quite a few of the boys outside camp. Outside camp mortars and IEDs were an ever-present threat.

When there was a death or serious injury the whole camp would be shut down into what was known as 'Op Minimise'. When Op Minimise kicked in, the Internet and phone lines would be shut down and there would be no communication with the outside world. This would ensure they could inform the family of the deceased or injured before you rang up your own family and said: 'Somebody died here last night and I know who it is.'

Op Minimise happened regularly during the worst times. And quickly I learned the signs that there was bad news coming. The office would go a bit quiet beforehand, then the Commanding Officer would make a solemn announcement. Initially there were no names, only their Army numbers. Tears were rare – at least in public – but always there was an overriding sense of sadness that would spread throughout the camp. Often I felt: 'What a waste' and you felt for the families who would receive the news they would have prayed wouldn't happen.

The longest Op Minimise was in place after a huge IED absolutely destroyed a tank. It was miles from the camp, near Basra city, but still we all heard the bang. At first it was so loud that I thought the camp itself had been hit. We all waited for the mortar alarm to go off, but it didn't. The IED was so huge there was no chance of anyone surviving. Tragically, the whole team of four was killed, including a female soldier who was a friend of Prince William's.

For days afterwards the camp was locked down with no contact with the outside world and inside everyone was in mourning for the loss. Morale hit rock bottom after that as we all felt for their families. It hit the female soldiers even harder if there was a possibility that a woman was among the dead. You thought you knew the worst the insurgents could do and then they still had the ability to shock you with something as extreme and horrific as that.

That incident brought home to every one of us the horror of war. While we didn't know everyone who was killed, every death or injury affected us all as we realised someone's loved one was gone and we also knew that next time it could be someone we knew... or even ourselves. The truth was, life generally in Iraq was absolutely horrific. Aware they could be engaged at any moment by insurgents the guys faced nightmares on patrol. However, despite the threat of IEDs, snipers and mortar and rocket attacks, they unflinchingly served their country. Their courage is extraordinary and I have so much respect for them as it's such a hard job.

After a few weeks I was moved to another area of the camp, called Camp Charlie. There, I joined two other women inside one section of living quarters, made up of huge sand-coloured tents. Each of the shared living quarters was divided by a wooden wall so that you had privacy; a corridor ran the length of the tent. I was the only mum in my working group. There were three of us in my room: a forty-something flame-haired soldier called Debbie Hill, who was the bubbliest Territorial Army Private you've ever seen, and Corporal Sally Allison. They became two of my closest friends out there, along with another soldier, Corporal John Lewis, whose tent was nearby and who used to keep an eye out for us.

Unlike the Anderson Shelters, these tents had no overhead protection so the 'powers that be' devised a way for us to avoid getting shrapnel wounds if a mortar or shrapnel whizzed through them: we all had to build our own 'Concrete Coffin'. First, we were taken to collect a series of breeze blocks, which we then had to drag into the tent. Then you'd build yourself a two- or three-block high wall around your bed space. You were also offered a camp bed, but John explained to me that everyone turned it down and chose to sleep on the floor in their sleeping bag – the risk was that if a mortar bomb hit, the shrapnel could slice through the tent and kill you. So inside your Concrete Coffin you had more protection the lower to the ground you were – unless you took a direct hit, of course.

Inside our 'coffins' we were also handed a mosquito net and a hard mattress. Above the space you had to pin an A4 piece of laminated paper with your name, number and rank on it. That way, if anything happened to you, or if your accommodation was bombed, there would be a way of tracking who was supposed to be there. The coffin became home for the duration of my tour. To try and make it a little less grim I used Blu-Tack to plaster it with photos from home of Milly and little drawings and paintings she'd done at nursery. Everywhere I went, I always carried a photo of her under my body armour next to my heart.

Whenever I got a chance I'd ring home and tell Jamie what was happening and I loved to hear Milly's voice. 'I miss you and I'll see you soon,' I'd tell her. She used to say, 'I miss you too mummy.' It was so bittersweet, as while I was over the moon to hear from her my heart was breaking because I missed her so much. It was like a physical pain.

Mum also posted me a pink shower curtain, so I hung that makeshift over the top of my bed. It wouldn't have won plaudits as a design feature as it looked awful, but for me it was a reminder of real life back home.

Day to day, though, life was pretty grim. Showers and loos at Camp Charlie were worse than festival standard so you'd always wear flip-flops – even in the shower. There was a 'Portaloo man' also known as 'the sh*t man', out of earshot, who drove around with huge 'hoovers' that sucked the poo out of the loos each day. Often they were so full you'd have to kick the front of them to get the poo to settle so that you could sit on the toilet without it touching your bum.

The women had their own shower block, subject to there being running water. Even then you couldn't escape the reality of where you were. There was one occasion when Debbie and I were having a shower and the mortar alarm went off and we had to lie on the bathroom floor, lathered up, completely naked and then talk awkwardly to each other until the threat passed. We'd rather have our lives than our dignity.

Because it was so grim, something of a Blitz spirit existed around camp. Among fellow soldiers there was a strong sense of community and you'd soon get to recognise faces, although not every face was as welcome as others. For instance, every morning there was a little Iraqi guy who would stand outside the front of the female tent, holding two electrical wires. Each day we'd walk out on the way to breakfast and he'd say hopefully: 'Electrics?' He wanted to have a little wander through the female tent if someone gave him permission, probably imagining we had all kinds of flesh on show. But he never stood a chance of fulfilling his fantasy for we didn't even have electrics in the tents.

On another occasion an Egyptian contractor – so ironically, not a local – sneaked into our shower block and hid inside a cupboard. One girl screamed when she heard a noise and that dirty little man, realising he'd been rumbled, burst out from under the sink and scarpered. It was reported to the Royal Military Police and within an hour he'd been caught – security was so tight. He would have been sacked and that was the end of it. I always made sure I checked the cupboards in the shower block before having a wash after that.

After two months I'd fully grasped what being in a war zone is really like. Six people had died, and on the grapevine I'd heard that Allies had reportedly killed more than seventeen Iraqis directly involved in attacks on the camp or its residents. We were never told the full figures, but the camp rumour mill was rife with information about things that had taken place.

The weird thing about war is that you have spurts of activity, where you are running on adrenaline and you are full of fear and then there's a lot of downtime where you aren't really doing much and so you have to entertain yourself and it gets quite boring. The downtime is, in some ways, just as hard, as you are trying to process what is happening around you, but you can't as it's so extreme and you don't want to offload on each other as you might tip someone else over the edge. Debbie would try to devise mad ideas to keep everyone's spirits up. Along with her kit she'd managed to cram in a belly dancing skirt and she used to dance, jiggling her belly and bottom in the tent with the two of us – even though there was no music – to have us in hysterics and break the monotony.

Debbie was a beautician in Civvy Street and while she was a brilliant soldier she was also a girly girl like me, so when she discovered that Boots The Chemist would deliver to BFPO addresses she was the first to place an order. As a treat she ordered Veet cold wax – the stuff in the roll-on bottle – so that she could host a girls'-only waxing party. By then everyone was getting a bit of leg regrowth. As she was trained on the professional kit, she was confident that she could do the job.

On the night it arrived, I was first to have a go. Instead of a nice beauty parlour bed, she got me to lay on the dirt on the floor of the tent before she started rolling cold wax down my leg. I immediately started yelling – it was more painful putting the cold wax on than pulling it off. We started laughing so hard in the tent I was doubled over when the mortar alarm went off. Immediately the laughter stopped. We had to throw on our body armour and helmets and I lay there with half-waxed legs, thinking this wouldn't be a very dignified way to go. Then, as we continued to wait for the all-clear, I became desperate for the loo. You can't just stroll off to the toilet block when you are in the midst of a potential mortar attack so I had to grab a plastic bag and have a wee in it, while my legs were still sticky and covered in wax. It was a really undignified moment and afterwards I vowed never to have my legs waxed in a war zone again, but you can't be a princess over the call of nature when you are in a conflict zone.

Another issue was that tap water would regularly run out on camp as it was delivered by lorry each day and pumped into massive underground tanks. By mid-afternoon when everyone had showered, more often than not, the water was gone. So if you wanted to guarantee a shower, you needed to be up at the crack of dawn. If we didn't get up in time we found out a way to improvise: shower using bottled drinking water. We came up with the idea when Sally brought us all bright green face masks when she came back from two weeks R&R. After a lovely pampering session we went to the showers and there wasn't even a drop of water so we had no way of getting it off. So we improvised and stacked the bottled water in the forty-degree sun outside our tent, waited for it to heat up and then used it to wash it off. From that day on, if we missed the shower water, we'd have bottled water hot showers.

The pampering sessions may sound frivolous, but in reality they were anything but. They were a great way to keep your sanity in the pressure-cooker atmosphere and a real treat for we had nothing. Another time my mum sent some Boots No7 nail varnish, which became the most prized contraband in camp. Obviously, we weren't allowed to put nail polish on our fingernails but loads of the female soldiers had red toenails under their steel toe-capped boots. The ultimate in decadence, it was a way of keeping our spirits up.

A few months into my deployment Debbie also went home for two weeks R&R, where she dreamed up another morale booster. Not only did she come back with face cream, she also brought me a special gift: Norman the Gnome. My new friend, complete with a fishing line, stayed outside our tent for five weeks and even became an unofficial camp mascot.

One day we woke up and discovered that Norman had been kidnapped. Determined to repatriate him, we went to the Admin office armed with a photo of him and posted up missing posters all over the camp. Even the British Forces Radio got involved in a campaign to rescue Norman. After a week we received a phone call from the Quartermaster, saying: 'I think I've got something of yours here.' It turned out one of the little Iraqi guys had found Norman in a portable loo and thought he was there for the taking so had taken him home for this garden in downtown Basra. Then he'd seen the missing posters, panicked that he was going to lose his job as they were paid good money, so he came clean and brought Norman back, pleading not to be sacked.

So Norman once again lived quite happily on our doorstep for a few weeks until he was kidnapped again. This time we received a ransom note that he would only be returned if we delivered twenty-five cans of Coca-Cola. So we headed to the Naafi – the camp tuckshop – and left the drinks at a designated location. But we were double-crossed and Norman wasn't freed and all the Cola was pinched! We then started receiving letters from all over Iraq: including of Norman sat on a toilet, riding the top of a tank and even on R&R, back in Britain!

As we got further into my deployment the laughs became fewer as the camp began to receive more rocket and mortar attacks and one hit just outside of where I worked. Luckily I wasn't in when it happened but later on I saw my boss and he looked scared, the first time I'd ever seen him look like that, and it frightened me. It was clear to us all that had it been a different time of day there might have been a different outcome. Everyone realised they had a sell-by date and that no one could be confident they were 100 per cent safe. I knew I had to get on with the job I'd trained to do, but I hated it and I developed a cold sore from the stress of it all. We were in a constant state of extreme pressure and anxiety for we literally didn't know what was going to happen next. Morale was low and the only thing that kept us going was the fact that we all had each other and so we started to settle into some sort of routine. We were building a haphazard family and starting to make a life within the compounds of camp.

CHAPTER FIVE

CAMP LIFE
IN IRAQ

As the weeks passed, despite everyone's best efforts life at camp seemed to get tougher. I missed Milly and Jamie desperately. Some people may judge me for being a mum in a war zone, but my argument is what made me different from all the dads with babies and toddlers who were also serving out there? But it's fair to say that as a woman I was very much in the minority and as the only mum in my working group, there were times when I felt isolated as the other girls couldn't truly understand how I was feeling.

Debbie was in her late thirties and she had no desire to be a mum, and Sally also didn't want any kids at that point in her life, although she later became a mother. Although they'd often ask about Milly, they couldn't truly understand how my maternal instinct left me aching to be reunited with her. I thought I'd cope better than I did but it was like a physical pain. When I chose to have a child while serving in the Armed

Forces, I knew that one day I would face the prospect of leaving her, but the reality of it was much harder than I could ever have imagined. However, it was hard for the dads too. Being a woman didn't make me any different, it's just that, as a woman, I felt able to express my feelings much more than the men did for they'd often bottle it up.

Nevertheless, I carried a deep sense of guilt that I'd left her and that's something I still carry to this day. I never talked about Milly when I was on duty as it made the agony of being away from her too raw and I had to concentrate all my energies on the job at hand. During work times I had to force myself into Army mode and focus on the job I was trained to do and that included suppressing my 'mum' mode. But during free time everyone talked about life back home and being a mum led me to form a strong friendship with another clerk, Corporal John Lewis. Tall, bald and from Grimsby, he was married with one son, although he and his wife definitely wanted more, and we bonded over stories about our kids and better halves. Because his tent was directly next door to ours, he became our male escort after the laundry was taken and no one wanted to take any chances.

Letters and welfare parcels from home were central to the bond John and I forged. Collecting your post every couple of days was hugely significant, especially if you knew something was on its way out to you, as it gave you something to look forward to. Most of my post came as 'Blueys' – flimsy blue pieces of paper which would arrive after a two-week delay. And Jamie was amazing, writing to me daily. Every week he'd send a letter enclosing photos of Milly and little drawings he'd done with her. Nikki would regularly send me my favourite strawberry-flavoured jelly sweets, as well as a letter with all the latest gossip. In one package another friend sent me a female blow-up doll to join our 'women-only' tent. 'She' was soon nicknamed 'Mustafa Shag' by one of the lads!

While the funny gifts gave everyone a laugh, it was the letters that we all looked forward to the most. Often I'd sit down outside the post room with John and we would open our Blueys together before sharing our news from back home. Everyone took an interest in the drawings and letters from each other's kids – it was a little piece of normality and joy to share. I remember showing John a book Milly's nursery had sent me after she made it for me.

Then, when Mother's Day came, Jamie sent me a clip frame of photos of Milly and some art he'd done with her. I collected my parcel just before starting work with a real rough, tough soldier called Dave. As soon as he saw the wrapping, he said: 'Are you going to bubble?' which is what they call crying in the Army. I said: 'No, I don't have a clue what it is,' then I opened it and I just bawled. Dave half-groaned and half-laughed and then said: 'I knew you were going to do that!' He still wanted to see my latest photos of my little girl, though, so he was a big softy, really.

Jamie would also email me photographs of Milly all the time. As he'd been deployed before, he knew how important the post and parcels were as they connected you with your life back home. He also knew how little luxuries make a massive difference when you are on deployment, so the minute I needed anything he'd get it straight in the post – including a dressing gown, and some crisps or other treats. One time I ripped my pajamas so I emailed him, saying: 'please can you send me some new ones' and he went straight to the shops and it was done right away.

A massive pastime was poker as the camp was dry and it was an easy way for people to occupy their minds. We played for POGS, which is a form of plastic currency as no one used small change on camp. If you paid for something at the Naafi using a dollar note, instead of getting cents you'd be handed POGS, which were little round discs that had the amount such as fifty cents or seventy-five cents written on them; this made sense as logistically the Army would struggle to carry enough loose change to support camp with so many people coming and going.

For each hand we'd play five cents in POGS, which was little more than two pence. John tried his hardest to teach me but I was rubbish. One day when we were playing I was completely down in the dumps and John asked: 'What's up, Hannah?' I told him that it was Milly's birthday the following day and although I'd sent a card, I just felt awful I wasn't going to see her. John and some of the chefs at the canteen then hatched a plan and decided to bake an iced cake, which said: 'Happy Birthday Milly'. They all sang 'Happy Birthday' and we celebrated, albeit from thousands of miles away. Of course that had me in floods of tears that they could do something so touching. There was no such thing as Skype on camp and none of us ever sent photos home – I only wanted to do that when I was safe and sound back home. But we could ring home. You'd get thirty minutes every two weeks to use on a phone card. But the lads were amazing and a lot of them would let me use up any spare minutes they had to ring Milly, which was such an extraordinarily generous thing to do.

As well as admin one of my other roles was guard duty at the local prison – a vast, grey concrete bunker on the furthest perimeter of Camp Charlie. Women soldiers were in short supply and I was told someone would be 'dicked' (Army slang for picked for the job) unless there was a volunteer. Keen to get out of the office, I put my hand up.

Each morning I'd be picked up by a Sergeant Major in a Land Rover and driven over to the prison, five minutes' drive from the centre of Camp. By the time we arrived, shortly after dawn, there would be a long queue of burka-clad women waiting to see their husbands. Some of them simply wanted to come and visit, but others had an ulterior motive – they wanted to build bombs or smuggle other contraband. Blowing up the prison so they could get out was the ultimate goal for some extremists, so they would sneak in a baby's nappy, a switch or a tiny amount of explosives. It would all come in dribs and drabs.

Due to their beliefs, the women could not be searched by men and that's where I came in: makeshift tents were set up, where the females would all come to be checked, one by one. Translators would stand by us as we conducted searches, helping us tell the women what they needed to do. We quickly realised that when the translators didn't turn up for work, we needed to have our wits about us as it might be a sign the camp was going to be attacked. You'd still give the women a nice smile and motion to them to take off their shoes, or open their bags. Sometimes you could sense the ones who hated us and it was a game of cat and mouse.

Once, when I bent down in an unguarded moment to pick up a woman's shoes instead of getting her to hand them to me she grabbed hold of me by the hair and started swinging me around, leaving me screaming for help. Just outside the search tent were Welsh Guards with machine guns and it lasted just seconds, but it was enough to shake me up. The minute they entered, she let go and so despite her vicious assault there was no retaliation. Her punishment was that she wasn't allowed in that day – we had to be better people than they were – although I never made that mistake again.

There are certain things, like that incident, that really hit home but you have a little cry, dust yourself off and then get on with it. But it was our world and there was no escaping it so the only way to survive was to go numb to what we were being subjected to at the time. That's why when they get back home it's often hard for soldiers to adjust – they've had to switch themselves off for six months in order to get through. Many of the women brought babies or toddlers to the prison with them. Kids are just kids and they don't care if you are in the Army or not. They'd smile merrily and as a mum I always wanted to be as gentle and friendly as I possibly could.

But the reality of how vital our role became was brought home to me during one routine search when a mother brought along her child, wearing combat trousers. There were so many little pockets it took ages to search him and to ensure he wasn't scared, I remember tickling him and talking to him and smiling to put him at ease as I checked each and every one of them. Then, inside a pocket I found something and pulled out a tiny switch with a little wire. Initially I thought: 'What is that?' assuming it might be a toy. Then, as I examined it more closely, it slowly dawned on me that it could be something far more sinister. I shouted to the armed guard, who came in and then called his Sergeant Major. He looked at it, then turned to her and said, 'This is potentially a switch so you are not coming in today.' That was it – she was turned away and the switch, which we feared could potentially be used in a bomb, was confiscated. She was entitled to her human rights and visiting rights just as we are over here, so the guard commander decided to let her go.

I was appalled and sickened that any mother would use her child, her own flesh and blood, as a smuggling mule, especially when it was potentially such a horrifying reason. There was no outward sign whatsoever of what she was concealing and there's no doubt she would have come back, although I personally never saw her again. The flip side of it is that sometimes these women did things involuntarily. She may not have wanted to do it – someone could have threatened to kill her child, so you can't judge when you don't know the full story. I have no doubt some of the people did things because they were bad and because they believed in the cause they were fighting for at the time. Equally, others were threatened or put under pressure and they felt they had no choice.

One of the more bizarre aspects of the prison guard duty was that the women were allowed to bring in pans of food for the prisoners. We were supplied with hand-held metal detectors so we could scan all the food and if we had any doubts we would stir it up with a spoon, or even feel around inside with gloved hands to make sure nothing was concealed. One day a woman showed up with a boiled dog's head in a metal dish, still with its eyeballs intact, which made me want to retch. Because its skull cavity was such a good potential hiding place we had to get the gloves and metal detector on the dog and it stank, which wasn't nice at all.

Once they were all inside the prison we would stand on concrete plinths to guard throughout the visiting time and watch individual visitors. Each family would sit on mats and have picnics huddled in groups and we'd each be tasked with watching certain groups to ensure there was no threat or to diffuse fights breaking out because of hierarchical disputes as there was a definite pecking order among the detainees. Fortunately I never got caught up in one in the prison, but there were protocols in place. The armed guards on all the doors would grab the back of the soldiers body armour who was on guard inside – which would have included myself – then they'd pull you outside, walking backwards, so you faced the enemy at all times and then they would shut the doors and and lock you all in for the duration of the fight.

Even back on camp if you were on guard duty there were still risks. The camp was vast and at night some areas of it were pitch black, where there were no tents, so you'd be completely alone. One of my greatest fears was being caught on my own in one of those areas in a mortar attack at night. I don't know what I would have done. I was told there had been a sniper taking pot shots so everywhere you went, you had to wear body armour, and jogging around the perimeter was banned as a result.

One of the lads had a legendary escape near the perimeter boundary that became the stuff of camp folklore. He was standing having a cigarette, waiting for a transport vehicle, when someone fired a mortar bomb that, by chance, hit the ground right next to him. Though it left a crater, incredibly it didn't detonate. It was a miracle he lived to tell the tale and his survival spread like wildfire around camp. A real brush with death, it totally shook him up. The bomb disposal team had to go out and do a controlled explosion. It was unbelievable. But incidents like that made us all realise that if it's not your time, it's not your time.

Three months into my deployment I had two days of

Operational Stand Down – which meant I had completely free time. A group of us, including Sally and John, decided to take one of the regular military flights that went to Kuwait to get away from the pressure-cooker atmosphere of the camp. I was so excited that I couldn't sleep the night before, knowing I was going to get out of the shithole of camp. Of course I'd rather have been going home, but this was the next best thing.

But first we had to get out of Basra. It was full kit and helmets for the two-hour flight, again under cover of darkness. Landing at the US Air Base in Kuwait called Camp Arifjan at 5am, we headed straight for breakfast after a quick change and a wash. We were all caught up in a holiday atmosphere. Relief washed over me that I was away from Iraq – albeit for just forty-eight hours. Camp Arifjan was probably the most luxurious and vast I'd ever seen. Compared to our facilities, the US cookshop was like a five-star hotel and the breakfast buffet had everything and anything you could think of, just like a five-star Hilton. I chose sausage, pancakes and syrup and sat in air-conditioned luxury within a proper building, not a stifling tent.

By contrast, the meals at our British camp were notoriously terrible as everything was shipped in from outside Iraq for there was a threat of poisoning if it was local. Staples were tinned fruit salad and while there was a hot breakfast option of bacon and eggs, because the cookhouse was in a tent there were flies everywhere. The most appetising thing on the menu was the cereal miniboxes flown in from the UK and served with UHT long-life milk. You'd struggle to survive more than a hastily eaten meal as the air conditioning buckled under the heat from the stoves. Dinners were often stews made from canned meat and always there were loads of chips. Whenever a delivery came in there would be salads and fresh fruit, but here in the US camp everything was on offer, like an all-you-can-eat banquet. The British camp was a poor relation in comparison. Our two main luxuries were a small Naafi, which had a limited selection of crisps and sweets, and a professional Mr Whippy ice cream machine, which boosted morale more than anything else when it was flown in. They'd pour the mixture in the top and the machine did the rest. In the searing heat it was a massive treat. The Americans had Starbucks coffee, burgers, pizza and pretty much everything you could wish for, which was extraordinary. After we'd eaten so much our stomachs hurt, we decided to leave the base, get a taxi and hit the malls.

Switching off completely from the hell of Iraq was bliss. I put on the only civvies I had with me: filthy brown combats and a black T-shirt. I'd never been anywhere like Kuwait, which is a beautiful country, dripping in wealth. It was a world away from where we'd been and it felt much richer than our own country. There was a sense of unreality – we had just stepped out of a war zone and now we were able to jump in a taxi, stop for coffee and walk freely and without fear. Even using a cashpoint machine felt like a treat.

The streets were lined with more Ferraris than I'd ever seen in my life and I wandered from shop to shop looking in the windows, admiring the latest fashions and drinking in the normality until we found a Debenhams, the only store we recognised from the UK. Inside it was exactly like the shops at home, except the clothes were more modest, with long sleeves and dresses and skirts that would cover legs. Desperate to take off our dusty clothing we all splashed out and bought a change of clothes each. I chose a bright pink kaftan so my arms were covered, and a pair of long shorts, along with a modest black swimming costume as we planned to visit a water park the following day.

We'd arranged to stay at the US camp as it catered for Allied troops who were moving forward to other countries and when we discovered the American soldiers had a line dancing night, it only added to the surreal atmosphere. We stayed up all night before heading to Kuwait's biggest water park and had the time of our lives there, whizzing down water shoots, diving and swimming and generally letting our hair down. All the women were in burkinis but no one bothered us and we had an amazing time – mostly because it was in such stark contrast to where we'd been.

That night we dined at the exclusive Kuwait Towers. Eating amazing food, although there was no alcohol, we gazed out at the views across the city. It was spectacular, but all I wanted was to have Jamie and Milly with me, and the elephant in the room was that we had to go back. We crammed a two-week holiday into forty-eight hours, staying out until literally ten minutes before we had to be at camp for the flight back, dressing again in full kit in case we faced an attack.

Within hours of flying back to Basra I was brought back down to earth with a bump. Talking to Sally, while I was ironing my kit for the next day in our tent, gossiping about our break, we were interrupted by a distinct whistling over our heads. 'What was that?' I said and she said: 'It must have been a helicopter or something.' With that, there was an absolutely enormous bang and dust flooded into the tent. Everything that we owned fell to the floor. My ears were ringing – it was such an enormous boom. A mortar had sailed over the top of our heads and landed close enough to shake the ground around us. With that, the mortar alarm went off.

That night, the camp took such a pounding from too many mortars to count. Hit after hit, it just went on and on. We all put on our body armour and helmets and lay inside our concrete coffins, praying for it to stop. Every time another mortar went off, I shook more and more, just waiting to get blown to smithereens. I grabbed one of the photos I kept of Milly beside my bed and I looked at her, praying the onslaught would end.

After forty-eight hours of relative normality I found the whole experience overwhelming. I'd never known fear like it. I kept inwardly repeating to myself: 'Please let it pass' and I tried to focus on Milly's smile when we were reunited, but as the bombardment became more intense I started sobbing. I knew that people were dying. Reality had dawned by that point that there was a chance I might not make it home to my family. I became acutely aware of the fact that I was in my early twenties and of my own fragile mortality.

During a brief lull my friend Sally crawled over and lay inside my breeze blocks with me. Cuddling me, as much for her own comfort as mine, she said, 'Are you alright?'

Desperate, I replied: 'I'm not going to get home from here and I've got a two-year-old daughter.' Inconsolable, I just couldn't shake a terrible feeling that something bad was going to happen to me and I was genuinely scared witless. Somehow I'd managed to pull myself back together by the time the onslaught ended. I'd had my self-pitying moment and now I had to get over it and get on with the job I'd been trained to do.

But after Kuwait it was just incredibly hard to get back

into the mindset of being in a war. When the mortars stopped flying, our ordeal didn't end. Members of the ordnance team started walking round the perimeter of our tent. We could see their feet and the flash of their torches and they kept saying: 'Stay down! Stay down!' as the all-clear hadn't been given.

'What do you think they are doing?' I asked Sally.

'They are looking for unexploded devices,' she replied.

So they must have counted the incoming devices and realised there was an unexploded one somewhere. We lay there in fear that it would detonate before they got to it. I don't know if they ever found anything – thankfully it wasn't around the perimeter of our tent, but that was the worst attack I ever experienced and it was so traumatic that I remember it like it happened yesterday.

It was so bad that my boss, who was much older than me, came to find me to check that I was OK. He gave me a big hug and said: 'Are you alright?' My eyes welled up as I said: 'No.' So we went outside with some of the lads for a cigarette to calm our jangling nerves and then we got hit again so we all had to lay on the ground until it was over.

Because I'd had my tears I was OK for that second attack, but one of the lads afterwards couldn't light his cigarette as his hands were shaking so much. He kept saying: 'Fucking hell, I can't believe this is happening!' and his adrenaline was going, whereas my tears had been my release. I grabbed hold of his fingers to steady him and used my lighter to spark him up.

I realised then that the lads felt exactly the same fear as I did – it's just that they often bottled it up and that's why, when they got home, they struggled more in some ways to come to terms with what they'd gone through. When the bombing ended, and after seeing his reaction, I couldn't help but think of the young boys who had to face so much and that it included potentially facing down insurgents every time they left camp. Even though everyone believed at that time we were in Iraq for the right reasons, I felt it still must be hard to deal with.

When Op Minimise was lifted a day later I rang my dad. For weeks I'd been coming to the realisation that my chances of getting out unscathed were diminishing day by day. I remember sobbing down the phone: 'Dad, you need to get me home. I'm going to die out here. I don't care how you do it but you've got to get me back.' I hadn't told them how bad things were before, but now I was scared and I wanted to go home. It had been easier not to tell them about it beforehand as I didn't think they'd understand, and also I was worried about worrying them. For that reason I went for weeks without emailing as I didn't want to lie, or I'd write funny stories about the Portaloo man to avoid talking about what was happening.

Dad told me afterwards he was worried but he didn't let me know it. 'Don't be silly, you can't be a deserter, you need to do the job that you have trained to do. You are out there to help Iraq. You will be home on R&R soon and you will be fine,' he said to reassure me. I remember repeating: 'You don't understand. I'm going to die out here. I'm not going to come home. There's been a terrible mortar attack, people have died out here.'

At the time they dismissed it as just a really bad day and that I was having an emotional outburst. Inside they were worried sick and every day Mum would check the news the minute she got home from work to see if there had been any explosions, injuries or deaths. For the months I was out there she feared hearing on the news: 'Someone has been killed but the family have not yet been informed.' But Dad's words made me get myself together. I hoped that in some small way I was helping to make a difference to innocent people out there, perhaps even a child like my own daughter.

Over time I got used to the rockets. Sometimes I even thought I preferred it when there was lots incoming – at least we knew what they were up to. I even managed to sleep through some of the alarms at night, although I don't know whether that was a good thing or not. Camp life wasn't all bad.

One of the highlights was a Saturday night on camp. The camp was dry – meaning there was no alcohol – but after the pounding I decided we needed a drink. I had a rare day of stand-down over the following twenty-four hours and I knew I would have no responsibility the next day, so I asked one of the locals who worked on camp, who had tried to sell me booze previously, to get some for us. I paid him in dollars and the following day, he walked up to me with my contraband: a litre-sized bottle of Smirnoff vodka, which I concealed in my tent.

That night everyone had the same aim: to have a toast to friends and try to forget the shit of where we were. Quickly quite tiddly, I decided to wander over to a social tent. John spotted me giggling while he was playing cards with a senior officer and immediately knew something was up. He quickly threw in his hand and got me out of there the moment he smelt booze on my breath. I'd only had a little tipple, but if I'd been caught, there would have been a strict punishment for flouting the rules. Thanks to John no one spotted me and that was the only time I broke the no-alcohol rule.

In May 2007 I became aware via my colleagues that a VIP

would be arriving through my primary role in OPLOC. The VIP had to be signed in and out of Theatre, just like everyone else. News of a mystery arrival spread like wildfire around camp as all the lads had to put up green netting the length of the perimeter fence, just in case an insurgent sniper decided to try to take a pot shot from outside.

When the VIP arrived, it turned out to be Tony Blair, on what was to be his final tour of Iraq as Prime Minister. While I saw his entourage, I didn't clap eyes on Blair himself, as we weren't allowed close enough, but through the office I knew when he was expected to be checked out of Theatre. While he was there, the camp experienced a mortar attack, so he had a proper taste of what it was like. He ended up leaving earlier than we had anticipated but whether that was for operational reasons (timing it earlier than it was supposed to be, just in case someone tried to attack the plane) or due to the mortar attack, I suppose I'll never know.

While the PM was a diversion from the monotony of camp life, without booze we also invented other ways to let our hair down. John decided to host a fancy-dress night to boost morale, so thirty of us all got dressed up from odds and sods we managed to salvage from around the camp. I was a fairy made out of old ration boxes covered in tin foil and my pink shower curtain; John dressed as a hula girl, with two paper bowls covered in brown camouflage cream as his 'coconut bra', along with a 'grass' skirt made of mine tape. Even 'Mustafa Shag' was dressed and put in an appearance during the night! It was brilliant seeing everyone dressed up in their costumes. Two of the guys brought along guitars, followed by someone with a battery-powered iDock, so we had music.

Ironically, it was my friendship with John that ultimately

changed my life. As I explained earlier, when he told me that he was at the end of his six-month deployment and could get home early to his wife and son I didn't hesitate to volunteer to cover his duty. I wouldn't have got through my tour without John so I was really happy to help him, perhaps more so than for anyone else on camp. Whether it was bad luck or fate, that decision changed the trajectory of my life. Shortly after the duty started, the building I was standing in took a direct mortar hit. There was no warning, the building was flattened and I was buried, alive and alone, beneath it.

CHAPTER SIX

AFTER
THE BLAST

It's the call every parent who has a son or daughter serving abroad dreads. Just after midnight, Jamie rang my parents at home in Cumbria and his voice cracked as he told my dad: 'I'm so sorry but Hannah's been injured. She's alive but it's bad.'

The Army had wanted to send someone to knock on their door, but instead of sending the local police, as there was no barracks nearby, Jamie wanted to break the news himself. Mum has always been stoic and she was immediately practical: 'What can we do?' was her first response. They would have been prepared to fly out to Iraq if that were possible, as they just wanted to be with me.

Jamie said: 'For now, we can only wait. All I know at the moment is that she's very seriously injured [VSI]. It's such early days they are still working on her at the hospital out there and it's going to take time before anymore information comes through. Let's just hope to God that she's OK.'

In Army speak there are various grades of injury and the first is Casualty, which is generally not too bad. After that, there are three further grades of injury, where your next of kin would need to be informed: Serious, Very Seriously Injured, and Death. Jamie and my dad were aware that VSI meant they weren't talking about a scratch, but thankfully Mum had no idea of the significance of those three words.

The time spent waiting was the worst of their lives. They didn't sleep; it was agonising waiting for the next piece of news to drip through. Once she knew I wasn't flying home for forty-eight hours Mum decided to go into work, just to occupy her mind. She was so ashen that as soon as the head teacher saw her, he called her in and said, 'I can tell by your face that something is terribly wrong.'

As soon as Mum told him, she was given time off indefinitely to help look after me, no questions asked. Meanwhile, Jamie had to get Milly up and break the news. He said: 'Mummy is coming. She's been hurt in an accident but she is coming back to see us.' Afterwards he told me that it was gutting to try and prepare her, while not scaring her about what was going on.

I remember nothing of the ten-hour flight back to RAF Brize Norton, apart from briefly stirring and being patted on the hand by my nurse. As I was wheeled off the plane I woke up again. Being back on British soil felt so good as I knew I was finally safe, but I was desperate to see my family and I was disappointed they weren't standing there on the airfield, waiting for me. An ambulance was instead waiting on the tarmac and I was taken, with sirens blaring, to Selly Oak Hospital in Birmingham and put into a side ward as I was the only woman soldier injured at the time, and hooked up to countless machines.

I hadn't looked at myself in the mirror since the field hospital in Iraq and I was scared as to what everyone would think as I knew I was a mess with thirty stitches in my face and my leg so swollen, cut and bruised that I couldn't even bear a sheet touching it. Doctors had to work on me first, checking all my vital signs, plugging me into machines and drips of antibiotics and pain relief, and generally sorting me out.

Jamie walked in first with Milly. The left-hand side of my face, which was swollen and full of stitches, was the nearest to the door and as she toddled into the room, she didn't recognise me. That was gutting.

'Milly, it's Mummy,' I said. It broke my heart that she didn't know who I was. As soon as she heard my voice, though, she stopped dead in her tracks and stared. I nearly started crying because instead of running to me like she always did, she was scared because I looked so horrific.

I coaxed her by saying: 'Milly, don't worry, it's Mummy.'

She clung on to Jamie, who said: 'Don't worry, Mummy's a bit poorly but she'll be OK. Let's say hello.'

Finally, she came up to me and gingerly got up and lay next to me on my hospital bed. I'd dreamed of the moment I was going to see her when I got back from Iraq; she'd be in the crowds, waving a Union Jack and smiling, but this was nothing like that. Jamie was a rock, saying no matter what, he was there for me and we'd cope and face everything together, which reassured me, but Milly's reaction knocked me for six as it brought home to me just how bad things were. But I didn't cry because I knew I had to be strong for her, so we took some photos of me in bed next to her. In them, Milly's eyes are wild and terrified. It took her a week to come up to me without being scared, and even when I look at those photos now I feel not only devastation but above all guilt that my child went through that.

Once we'd spent some time together, the next person I desperately wanted to see was Mum and I got so distressed that I rang her, saying, 'Mum, where are you? You said you'd be here.'

She was frantic as she'd been held up in heavy traffic on the M6 and when she finally arrived, I started crying as she hugged and kissed me, saying: 'Hannah, I'm so relieved you are still alive.' She put her hand to my cheek and said: 'Hannah, you are going to be alright.' That's one of my strongest memories, as I desperately needed to hear those words from her.

Within hours I went down for surgery for the shrapnel wounds to my face and all my abdominal wounds, but because my foot was so mangled, they needed to let the swelling go down for at least two weeks before they could operate on it. Before I was taken down, Mum popped out to get a cup of tea and she was white when she came back.

'What's wrong?' I asked.

'I had to walk through the hospital and ward and it was the first time I have ever seen so many young amputees.'
Everything I had been through was hitting home, mixed with her relief that I was still there.

The next few days were gruelling as I had so many injuries a team of doctors, led by an extraordinary man, Professor Keith Porter, who was later given a Knighthood for his work, had to work through each and every one. There was barely a part of my body that hadn't been affected in some way by the blast. From the moment I'd arrived in Selly Oak I'd become aware that my hearing wasn't right and things were muffled, and also my vision was obscured. It's impossible to treat everything at the same time when you've suffered so many injuries, so doctors have to prioritise and treat the most serious first. I'd perforated both my eardrums, was left with just 20 per cent vision in my left eye due to retinal damage, a shattered foot, permanent nerve damage, a high-velocity shrapnel wound in my abdomen, facial scarring, a moderate brain injury, multiple flesh wounds that required surgery, a ripped-apart hand, a pole through my leg and face and countless other shrapnel wounds.

Each passing day seemed to bring a new diagnosis, so my list of injuries kept growing and growing. There were so many it was hard to keep track and to process exactly what I'd been through. They did an amazing job on my wounds. One surgeon had to do extra stitches in my face and he said to me: 'Whoever did this in Iraq did a wonderful job.' He promised his stitches were going just as well and he was as good as his word. My hand was heavily bandaged after they stitched it all back together and they also made it as good as new.

Jamie, Mum and Dad were just overwhelmed with relief that I was still alive but I was in deep shock as it slowly dawned on me how lucky I had been with such a huge number of wounds. I slept, on and off, for days due to the painkillers. I was overwhelmed by exhaustion as my body fought to recover, seeing only my family, who were my line to the outside world, making me laugh and giving me little snippets of gossip, which gave me respite from my pain.

I had a phone by my bedside and when it rang, four days later, I almost thought I was dreaming. When a male voice said: 'Hannah, it's me,' I had to think for a second about who was on the line. 'It's John,' he continued and I realised then it was John Lewis, with whom I'd swapped guard duty in Iraq. From the moment he'd heard I'd been blown up, the day after it happened, he'd been worried sick and I was so pleased to hear him, although I was drugged up to the eyeballs on morphine.

He asked me how I was and when I admitted: 'I've been better, but I'll get there,' he became quite choked up.

He said: 'I've got to say this to you, Hannah, I'm just so sorry as I know this shouldn't have happened to you. I feel so awful that you did such a good thing for me and now this has happened.'

I said: 'John, there's absolutely nothing to feel sorry for', and I meant it. I've never regretted swapping guard shift as he was a good friend to me, and that's what you do in the Army – you look out for your own. No one in the British Army was to blame for what happened; the blame for what happened to me fell squarely at the feet of the insurgent who fired the mortar that blew me up. I hate him. Everyone has free will and he could have chosen not to do it. I still feel anger that he's out there somewhere with no idea of the destruction and pain he has caused.

Mum, Dad, Jamie and Milly were constantly by my side during those first days. So they were as delighted and touched as me when, later that day, I also had a really special visitor who instantly had me in floods of tears, or 'bubbling' as he'd say. Karl, who'd pulled me from the rubble in Iraq, knocked on the door to my room and limped in with a big smile, carrying a huge teddy bear. Just the sight of him set me off, partly out of relief that he was OK. He was pretty battered from the blast; he'd suffered some serious shrapnel wounds and seeing him again took me right back to the moments beforehand when we'd shared a cigarette and had a laugh. It seemed a lifetime ago and neither of us had had any idea of the impact those few seconds would have on our lives. I realised it must have been him that I'd seen on the plane as he said he'd come back at the same time as me. He'd tried to see me several times, but each time I'd either been in surgery or asleep.

He said: 'I've been worried sick and I'm so, so sorry.'

I started crying really hard as I said: 'Thank you for getting me out of there', for Karl was the man who saved my life. He was so close to losing his own life that day and even though he'd also been badly wounded by shrapnel, he still dug me out of the rubble. It was an heroic act, and for me, Karl is an incredible man. From that moment on I always felt a special bond with him because he was the only man who had a real insight into what happened and we both suffered in the aftermath.

Mum then asked to speak to him for a moment outside my room. As they stood on the ward outside, she told him: 'Thank you for pulling my daughter out and getting her home to me.' Karl also gave Milly the teddy bear, which we still treasure to this day. It meant a great deal that he had come to see me as I'd wondered how he was and to this day I feel such immense gratitude that he pulled me from what would otherwise have been my grave.

During those first six weeks I had so many operations I lost count. They ranged from minor extra stitches to my face and smaller wounds under local anesthetic to major operations on my hand. Surgeons also continued to clean out shrapnel injuries on my abdomen and leg, and pump me full of nuclear-strength antibiotics. I was in a cycle of surgery, recovery and then I'd have another procedure. I was pretty out of it a lot of the time as I was taking all kinds of drugs and I wasn't really engaging in life. It was like I was in a bubble: distant from everything with the painkillers and other drugs acting as a warm, fuzzy cushion from reality. To be honest, that was a blessing at the time.

I also underwent scans for the bleed on my brain. As soon as I could manage it, I was attached to a special machine that sent ice down to a custom-made boot, which was used to try to reduce the swelling of my foot so they could operate. After three weeks they decided they would try to operate on it for the first time. I was full of optimism that they could put things right, but it wasn't to be.

Afterwards, my surgeon said he had to be honest and that he was gravely concerned. 'Your foot is terribly injured and while we will try everything we can, there's no guarantees about what the future holds,' he told me.

In my head amputation was not even in the equation and I was prepared to go to whatever lengths were necessary to save my foot and leg. When I told him that, he nodded and promised he'd try everything and explore every avenue possible for me. He warned that it would be a long haul with no guarantees of success, though.

While I was in hospital I managed to go short distances on crutches and when I finally got out of my side room, I saw some of the guys who had lost limbs or had suffered terrible burns and I was relieved I didn't face the same as them. They were absolutely amazing and they would whiz around the corridors of Selly Oak, getting on with it, but I remembered the doctor's words at Basra's field hospital and thought: 'I'm glad that's not me.' I still thought I was going to be OK in the end and the failed op was a temporary blip.

After six weeks, with the exception of my foot, my other

injuries had healed well enough for me to be discharged home until surgeons could operate again to try and pin my foot back together again. The bones were all floating around and they struggled to find an anchor to piece parts together again. On the morning I was discharged home I was ecstatic. A nurse helped me pack up my toiletries, magazines and loads of 'Get Well' cards I'd received. Raring to go, I was ready long before Jamie arrived to pick me up.

As soon as I arrived home my bubble of excitement burst. I couldn't even get down the stairs without him supporting me and once I was out of the cocoon of the twenty-four-hour care at the hospital and back at home, my life fell apart. Somehow I was supposed to use crutches to get around but I couldn't manage and so I became housebound, able to do little more than move from room to room, permanently in terrific pain.

I wasn't provided with a proper wheelchair because I hadn't been categorised as officially disabled yet as I still had both my legs. Normally, things like that are sorted out by Headley Court, the rehabilitation centre, but I never made it there for years as I was always having an operation or recovering from one. So basically, I slipped through the net. After two weeks, things were so desperate that Jamie asked the Red Cross to donate me a wheelchair.

The truth is I didn't want to be in a wheelchair full stop, and I was proud so I didn't want to ask for a handout. Jamie persuaded me 'needs must' and so I swallowed my pride as the situation was desperate. I told myself I wouldn't need it for long but as the wheelchair was so old and the house wasn't properly adapted I couldn't get it over the steps to get outside unless I hobbled up the stairs on my crutch and Jamie carried it out for me and then pushed me where I needed to go. We also had to move the furniture and I scraped the paint off the walls in the hallway with my wheels. Being sedentary meant I ballooned and my weight crept up from nine stone towards my peak weight of twenty-one-and-a-half stone within months.

The Army were great at supporting me financially and within months I received a compensation payment for my initial injuries. I was still on full Army pay, although I was on long-term sick leave, and it enabled me to pay off my credit cards and debts as well as put down a substantial deposit on a house in Winchester, which I planned to move into when I completed my Army career.

But in other ways, things initially weren't so good.

I was on two strong opiate drugs, oral morphine and fentanyl lollipops, which are normally given to terminal cancer patients to help ease their pain. The only time I've seen someone else use them is in the pictures taken when reality star Jade Goody was dying from cervical cancer. They are supposed to be much stronger than the morphine and I used them for a quick burst of pain relief when the morphine wasn't working. You let them dissolve on your teeth and your gums – they make you feel like you're not really there.

I wasn't functioning as when I wasn't consumed by pain, I was off my face on the drugs and I could barely look after myself, never mind be a mum. The most painful thing of all is that I became redundant as a mother. I was in so much pain, I couldn't lift Milly, I couldn't take her to the park or nursery; I couldn't even give her a bath or put her to bed. Jamie had to do it all, and in addition to everything else he became my carer. He'd get home from work, take off his jacket and then he'd start all over again. It was a living nightmare. I'd force myself to manage the toilet on my own but I could only have a bath when he was in the house. I'd always loved a good soak with bath oil and candles and at first I was so determined to try and help myself that I used to drag myself in and out of the bath even if it took hours, as I didn't want to be completely dependent on him. Other times, I was in so much pain I had to let him help me get in and out, and he'd even help towel me off while I kept my balance on my one good foot, holding the sink. I used to love relaxing in the shower as well, but I couldn't take them because I couldn't stand up anymore. No woman wants to ask her partner 'Please can you help me take a bath', and I found all the little losses of independence that were mounting up extremely hard to bear.

He did all the housework, dusting, hoovering and ironing, even doing the dishes as I sat there and watched him helplessly, hating every minute. I couldn't reach the hob, so he cooked. We put the kettle on a coffee table so I could make myself a drink without the risk of tipping scalding water down myself, but that was about the only thing I could do independently. One thing I could do for myself was crawl upwards on my knees and slide downstairs on my bum, holding my injured leg out in front.

Besides that, Jamie helped me to get dressed and undressed, peeling my skirt over my head so it didn't touch my leg. I lost my dignity at that point. To Jamie's credit he never once complained. He was my rock and I realise now how strong a man he is to have managed. But I didn't cope at all, instead feeling embarrassment, shame and anger that I was now completely dependent on him. Over time our relationship as husband and wife began to slowly erode, but I was too wrapped up in my own selfish bubble of misery to even notice.

Every night he'd cuddle me until I fell asleep but I totally lost my confidence and wondered how he could ever find me attractive at the size I was. I felt a failure not only as a wife but also as a mother as my life consisted of sitting in the house staring at the four walls or crawling around while I waited for my next operation. At first I'd crawl upstairs when Jamie was giving Milly her night-time bath, thinking even if I couldn't help, at least if I was there watching and talking to her then I was a part of it. As I sunk deep into a depression, I didn't even bother to do that anymore. Instead I'd sit downstairs. I didn't even cry that often – I just felt numb with it all.

On top of everything I started to suffer from Post-Traumatic Stress Disorder (PTSD). Night after night I'd cower underneath our bed screaming, convinced I was in the middle of a mortar attack. Luckily toddlers sleep like the dead and Milly never woke up. Later she often heard me screaming in pain, but Jamie and I protected her from the worst of my PTSD. Even though I was in the grip of it, my maternal instinct to protect her remained strong. To me the nightmares would seem completely real and even though I was in my bedroom, I'd be convinced I was back in Iraq.

During the daytime, whenever I was alone, I developed an obsession about watching videos of explosions in Iraq on YouTube. Hour after hour, I'd replay them again and again. It was like a form of self-harm; it would trigger me into reliving the horror of being buried alive in the rubble. I also became hyper-aware of Milly, convinced there was some unknown and unseen threat that would hurt or kidnap her. Unable to switch off the adrenaline, I was constantly in a state of fight or flight.

The reality is I'd become mentally ill. My thoughts weren't making sense and I was wrapped up in depression and misery, which in turn turned me into a selfish person. My mental health problems literally fed my weight gain. Along with steroids and the other cocktail of drugs I was taking, I pigged out and continued to balloon. During the lonely hours when Jamie had dropped Milly off at nursery and while he was at work, I'd wheel myself backwards and forwards from the fridge and kitchen cupboards to mind-numbing daytime TV shows. Binge eating to fill the bottomless pit of misery inside me, I'd think nothing of polishing off entire packets of chocolate digestives, six Penguin bars and an entire six-pack of Walkers crisps in a day. I didn't eat cereal, I couldn't even be bothered to make myself a sandwich; I just grazed and ate junk. And the more I binged, the fatter I became.

The Army did their best and they offered me help at every opportunity, but at that point they hadn't developed the incredible support systems that are in place now for casualties as the sheer number of injured troops that there are today didn't yet exist. The Army's support system has evolved so much that now they give you help before you even realise you need it. But back then, everyone did their best and they constantly offered me assistance, saying: 'What do you need?' But I didn't know what I needed and I was so insular and sick that I didn't want to ask for help. As the years passed I saw a dramatic improvement – and I got an incredible amount of help, without even having to ask. But at that point they were still learning how to help those who were still serving but had significant or life changing injuries.

Jamie did the shopping as I wasn't well enough to do it and he bought what I wanted. Struggling by then to keep his own head above water, he didn't even question me when I asked him to get more biscuits or even more of my favourite sweets, and because I was barely moving in my wheelchair, I just ballooned. After he'd been to work, bathed Milly and put her to bed and done the housework, Jamie would be too exhausted to cook, so he'd pop down the road to the camp chippie and buy a bag of chips or he'd order a takeaway curry or pizza each. I'd eat whatever it was and then gorge on a family bar of chocolate for dessert. In the grip of a food addiction, I was out of control and my appetite never seemed sated.

I didn't look in any of the big mirrors in the house because I didn't want to be confronted by what I'd become. Instead, I'd use a tiny, handheld cosmetic mirror in which I could only see part of my face so I wouldn't be faced with seeing how bloated I was.

The weight piled on at an extraordinary speed, in part due to the steroids I was taking. First, I went up from a size 10 to a 14, then a 16, then 20 and I ended up a size 24. I'd stand in the bathroom and when I saw the rolls of fat around my tummy and thighs I hated myself, but then I'd go down and open another packet of crisps. I felt so trapped in my body. My entire wardrobe hung unused.

I've always been a girly girl and when I was out of uniform I loved wearing beautiful bandage dresses, mini-skirts and knee-high boots. I had dozens of pairs of designer high heels too. Now the thought of getting into any of my Army uniform, apart from my beret, was laughable and I had to apply for an outsized one, which was utterly humiliating. I couldn't shop in normal shops anymore so everything was coming from plus-sized places and being bought online. If it was baggy and it was black, I would buy it.

For months I'd clung on to my wardrobe of size-10 clothes,

but once it became obvious I wasn't ever going to fit into them again I started throwing them out. It was awful and so depressing, like throwing away the real me. I was being attacked from all angles, it seemed. But what was even more depressing was seeing my clothes hanging there in the wardrobe as a reminder of what I once was. I just couldn't handle it, so they had to go. I remember throwing out the last of my smaller stuff – a Vivienne Westwood evening dress and a pair of skinny jeans – and just crying and crying about what had become of me and my life. I've always loved Michael Kors shoes and I got out my favourite pair of black high heels and just sat there, holding them and sobbing. I'd never wear them again.

But it wasn't about the shoes; it was about what I'd lost. I'd lost control of how I looked and I became so depressed I stopped wearing make-up. For days I went without washing, I completely lost my sense of identity and I hated myself and what I'd become. I felt very misunderstood and isolated as my whole life revolved around three things: TV, eating and my next hospital operation on my shattered leg. I'd always feel a sense of hope in the weeks leading up to the op that maybe this time something would go right for me, and then when it didn't, I'd be bereft all over again, feeling desolate when the pain didn't go away. I hid from my parents and family how dark things were. Even now, my mother struggles to understand how despite being such a close-knit family, I didn't ask her for help at that point, and when they wanted to help out at home I pushed them away. Even when they tried to talk to me about what I was going through, I got so angry and wouldn't speak to them about it. In fact, I hid from them the awful truth. I felt there was no point as there was no possible way they could understand. I was so bitter and twisted and angry that I'd become a shadow of my former self.

One of the few people I allowed near me was Nikki. She tried to coax me out of my misery and on one occasion she even managed to persuade me out of the house to go to a mess do. I just thought I couldn't buy anything nice as I was so big. Already I'd started covering up as much as I could; I didn't go out because of my size and I didn't want to meet new people because of it either. Nikki encouraged me to go shopping with her and helped me to buy a black dress.

Something happens when you are in a wheelchair: you become invisible to a lot of people. Some look at you surreptitiously; others talked to Nikki, or if I was out with Jamie, they'd speak to him. That has the effect of making you even more insular and pushing you into a little bubble, where you become a silent bystander of your own life. But with Nikki's help we found a lovely shop assistant, who helped us choose a half-flattering dress for me, even if it was the size of a tent. Then I started looking forward to not being in the house that night for the first time in ages. I made an effort and put on some make-up and she pushed me to the 'do' in my wheelchair. As she wheeled me in I felt insecure as I didn't want to be the fattest person in the room and the only person in a wheelchair, but everyone was a soldier or a soldier's partner so there was no one to be unkind.

I spent the night laughing at jokes but it was all a front and I behaved how I thought I was expected to behave. 'Maybe if I act happy that's how I'll end up feeling,' I thought, but in reality I was dying inside. Bless her, Nikki has always had my back and she knew how vulnerable I felt, so to cheer me up she started strumming an air guitar, using my crutches on the dance floor. It caused a few raised eyebrows among the higher ranks but she didn't care one bit. She was one of the people who kept me going. God, I don't know where I'd be without Nikki, Jamie and my family.

In total I had eighteen major operations to try and save my leg and many months of pain and rehabilitation after each one, but despite everyone's efforts, nothing was working and after each op I felt like I was back to square one again. It was soul-destroying. I was just thankful that I had my friends and family around if I needed them, so it was not only heartbreaking but also a massive shock to find out that stability was about to be wrenched from me again within weeks.

CHAPTER SEVEN

MOVING TO IRELAND

The only time I feel the Army truly failed me was in 2009. While I was still undergoing treatment and operations on my leg, out of the blue they told Jamie he was being posted for six months to Northern Ireland. I was devastated. I'd been on long-term sick leave, so when we were told we had to move within a month it was like they threw another grenade into the wreckage of our lives. I'm still angry after all these years that they did that at that time because it seems nothing short of stupid.

I was so poorly I contributed nothing to the move. The Army had a removal company who came in and packed everything up and unpacked at the other end. So while the mechanics of moving us over there were handled with typical military efficiency, what no one took into account was the devastating impact it had on our day-to-day lives. Nikki came over to see me just after James broke the news and I started sobbing, saying, 'I can't understand why they are doing this now.'

I felt so powerless. It was terrible as not only was I in agony and still in and out of hospital, but for the first time we would have no support from family and friends as we were so far from home. We'd only just arrived when members of Jamie's unit were shot by suspected IRA dissidents after ordering pizza delivery at Massereene Army barracks in Antrim, west of Belfast.

I was in hospital having a minor op at the time and I remember lying in bed, not being able to sleep and switching on Sky News and seeing the headlines that two soldiers had been killed. Still suffering from really bad PTSD, I was screaming and panicking and trying to ring Jamie as I was convinced it was him who'd been killed. I cried with relief when I finally got hold of him an hour later, but it was just such a stupid place to post us as a family after everything we'd been through and were still going through. When I look back on it now it seems insane that someone decided to ship us over there. I had around fifteen hospital admissions during that time and Jamie was just incredible at coping but it nearly broke us.

To be fair, the Army did all they could, and I would regularly get flown back by Aero Med with an escorted nurse every time I had a hospital appointment in the UK. But it was the isolation that broke us. Not only did Jamie do his job, he was looking after Milly as well over in Belfast and we'd lost the support network we'd had at home. He was my rock during that period and gave Milly the support and family life she needed. At that point he was also my lifeline to the outside world and he was my best friend in every way.

My injuries meant that intimacy was hard. Not only was I in agony, I felt like I was wearing a fat suit because my weight had ballooned so much. If I'm being honest, my mood swings were also so bad I wasn't a very nice person to be around then, but Jamie loved me anyway.

I remember one night he came home from work and I felt so isolated and alone I had a total mental breakdown fuelled by the PTSD and sheer quantity of pain-relieving drugs I'd consumed. I'd become convinced Milly hated me and I was an awful mum and so I just lost it, screaming and shouting as I felt the whole world was against me. But Jamie never once raised his voice to me: he just took it and was always so kind and understanding; he let me vent off. For months I was crying on him every single night when he came home from work as I couldn't believe my life had come to this. All the simple, little things we take for granted in life were gone.

Looking back now it seems incredible that Jamie and I had barely any outside help at all. We didn't even think to ask anyone at the hospital or in the Army if we could have a carer or a nurse to help me with the day-to-day stuff. It just didn't occur to me to ask for help because I wasn't disabled enough in government terms to qualify for help: in their eyes, I only had a broken foot. I didn't know my rights as a disabled person and looking back now I could, and should, have got some kind of care package.

The only good thing in Northern Ireland was that I had an amazing boss, who would come and pick me up in my wheelchair in his own Land Rover so I could come and sit in the admin office and just keep in touch with working life. Not that I ever did anything at all productive! But it was just the fact he took the time to come and get me. He showed me real kindness and he'd sit down with me and the other ladies in the office and we'd have a chat and a gossip. It made me feel there was life outside the four walls I was a virtual prisoner in. That small act of kindness made me feel human again and once I got to know them, a few of the women would even pop in and see me during the day. Clearly they all realised I was in a desperate place and they really did try to help me.

Apart from that, I was so low I just didn't want to socialise with people and I even pushed my own family away. They tried desperately to help but I wouldn't let them as I was so bitter and angry I almost wanted to be on my own and being so far away I was able to hide just how bad things had got. I was prescribed anti-depressants and at first I took them to try and take the edge off what I was feeling, but when I started to need stronger ones, I refused to take them as I didn't want to go down the route of self-medicating on top of the cocktail of drugs I had to take for the pain. I was in a vicious cycle and I couldn't see any way out. That's when I began to think of suicide as an option. I was just so low and I was getting into a darker and darker place.

I remember sitting in the bath one evening and thinking I could just go downstairs and take every single drug I owned and that would be it. Black, nothing, the pain would be gone and I'd finally get some peace. But always at the back of my mind I knew I had Milly and I couldn't leave her without a mum. It sounds awful to say but this made me feel worse as I felt so trapped and frustrated with my situation that I didn't even have the control over my own life to actually end it. I just felt so angry and bitter. Besides, I couldn't end it because of my responsibility not only to Milly but also to Jamie. If I'd killed myself then he wouldn't have been able to handle it either, but I was going downhill so fast at this point that I seriously considered it.

This period was the darkest of times for me. I wasn't coping with the pain, I wasn't sleeping with it, and I was literally going out of my mind. Our married quarters were right by the airport and every time I heard a plane go over the house during the night I was convinced it was a mortar attack. I'd scream and crawl down the side of the bed in terror. On one level I knew my PTSD was crawling its way back into my mind and I was trying desperately to fight it. On the other hand, at that point I can truly say my PTSD was beating me.

I felt I couldn't talk to anyone about how I was feeling because to admit I was struggling mentally would be an admission of defeat. The flip side was, I was just bottling everything up and then flew into terrible verbal rages. At some points Jamie couldn't even say hello to me without me getting angry. It was awful – I was a person I didn't recognise. I'd distanced myself from my family to such a point I felt I wouldn't have a second chance with them, which is absolutely ridiculous to think back on now. My mind was all over the shop. I felt like I was so trapped by life, my injury and the fact I had nobody else around me. But the reality was that wasn't the case at all: it was all in my head.

Poor Jamie had so much to deal with. He would suggest something to help, even going out for a breath of fresh air, and immediately I'd start shouting and screaming, abusing him verbally and just obliterating him as a person. I'm ashamed to say I flung in his face my decision to go to Iraq, shouting at him: 'You could have gone! It's your fault. You stood by and let me go.' That was never the truth and it hurt him, and I'm so desperately sorry I said that to him, but I was finding it really difficult to cope with what had happened to me. It's true that you lash out and hurt those you love the most.

The PTSD manifested itself with a growing number of obsessions at this point. I became convinced that I was dying or something terrible was going to happen to me; I also lived in fear someone was going to hurt me and I'd die. Another obsession developed that I had a brain tumour and I repeatedly went to my doctor at the medical centre. At night I'd insist a terrorist attack was imminent at the Army camp, and I'd sleep on the floor. The brutal reality was, Jamie was living with a lunatic.

Thankfully, it was Jamie who saved me from myself, recognising that what I was doing wasn't me and that I had all the symptoms of PTSD. Apart from Karl, he's the second man who saved my life. He turned to the Army for help and they immediately took it really seriously and I was given counselling and coping strategies. Many other serving and former soldiers struggle with their lives for many years after conflicts have ended, but the Army gave me expert treatment there and then. There is no cure, as PTSD changes the physical structure of your brain, but today, because of their help, I would be able to recognise it and would know how to deal with it if ever it threatened to come back.

Jamie carried on loving me even when I was screaming in his face about how useless he was; he just never stopped giving love. He just kept telling me that we would get through this and he would agree with me that it was shit what had happened and I had every right to be angry. Jamie has a way about him and one of his strengths is that he's so calm in a storm. I didn't know at that point, but, understandably, he was struggling as well with how dark our lives had become and what had happened to me. He was just so strong for me when I needed him most and held it all together for so long that I never knew and he never showed any of the suffering he was obviously going through. I don't know what I would have done without him. If he had been a lesser man he would have walked away.

Although things didn't work out in the end for us there's no doubt he is a great person and I'm so lucky he's Milly's dad. Ironically, things only got worse between us when things actually got better with my health; we had been muddling through in our current dynamic, so when things changed that's when the cracks began to appear. He wasn't my husband anymore: he had become my carer.

Perhaps my misery was written on my face because after eighteen operations in three years, Professor Sir Keith Porter at Selly Oak Hospital in Birmingham, whose medical care I had been under since day one, tentatively raised with me again the possibility of having my leg removed. He explained in such a gentle way that my situation would be improved as I might actually get mobility back as opposed to being in the awful agonising rut I was stuck in with my foot. It was a big decision, but after so many procedures, we both knew they had come to the end of the road. In my heart, I'd had enough as well – I couldn't stand the pain anymore. The minute he mentioned it as a real possibility for me a light bulb went on in my head. As I was on my own, he told me I had to talk to Jamie when I got back to Ireland and to think about it a lot.

The flight home to Northern Ireland went past in a blur because all I kept thinking about was the amputation and how despite me losing my leg I might actually have a chance of getting my life back. I couldn't go on anymore with what was happening, my weight was still creeping up and I was desperate to change all that.

Looking back, I also recognise that I was at the end of a

three-year grieving process. I had mourned not only for what my life 'should' have been but also grieved for my leg. I'd had tears, anger and now my leg was holding me back from living again. In my heart I now knew that the doctors had done all they could and unfortunately it wasn't getting any better. It was that fact which ultimately made my decision easy: I finally recognised that amputation was the light at the end of the tunnel. This time, I knew that was what I was going to do. It was as if something in me clicked. I made a decision there and then that I was going to be happy: it was that simple. Already I'd started to see what other soldiers were achieving. I decided to get myself in the best place possible because the moment my leg was amputated I wanted to hit the ground running; I wanted to get on with life. I'd grieved enough and I didn't want to do it anymore. For two years I'd virtually not had a leg anyway.

Jamie picked me up from the flight and I'd barely shut the door of the car when I told him about it. Immediately he said that he would support me if I decided to go for it. He'd seen other guys in his regiment who had had amputations and how well they were doing, and how not only had they got their lives back, they'd actually got a stab at a better life. One of the guys in Jamie's unit, who'd lost a limb in Iraq, actually got back to full service. He just kept saying to me: 'If you truly feel it's right you have got to do this, you have got to take the chance to change your life.' I knew with all my heart it was the right decision for me at that time. By the time we had completed the twenty-minute journey back to our house that was it, I was set on getting it done. With Jamie's help and backing I could do it and I felt it was my one chance to live again.

I called my mum the next day and told her I was going to have my leg removed and at first she didn't want me to do it. It was awful for me as I felt so responsible that I was making her feel bad and worrying her but I knew there was no other way back for me. I tried to convince her I was doing the right thing to give me a chance of living life again. She was just so worried about me. I think it was the thought of her only daughter actually choosing to do this to herself, but she didn't live in my head and she didn't live inside my body and didn't know the mental torture and physical agony I was going through every minute of every day. I think she still hoped, just as I once had, that my foot would get better.

I had pushed my family away to such an extent they didn't really know what was going on in my day-to-day life and just how depressed and suicidal I'd become. But the more I tried to explain on the phone to my mum why the amputation was a positive thing, the more she asked me to think about the long-term reality. I didn't want to hear that so I just got really angry with her and started shouting that she didn't know what the hell was going on with me so how could she have an opinion? In the end I slammed the phone down.

Looking back, I just think I felt terrible because I knew she had my best interests at heart. I lashed out because I felt trapped in an awful situation that had no easy solution or cure and the strain and the stress of it was horrific.

The next day I rang my dad while he was at work knowing that my mum wasn't there. I had an hour-long conversation with him and talked everything through calmly. The first thing I said was: 'Dad, Mum's so upset I need to speak to someone who can take the emotion out of this decision. I need to think and talk logically about it.'

119

The severity of the consequences of the amputation had now hit home and I was processing the negatives, not just the positives of what becoming an amputee actually meant in everyday life. Dad was brilliant. Together we talked through what I would do in old age, how I would go to the toilet, and actually what my life would become with only one leg. At this point I hadn't spoken to any other amputees so I didn't really have any points of reference on any of these types of questions.

While neither my dad nor I knew the answers it was brilliant to just have a sounding board to talk things through logically and calmly with. In my heart of hearts, though, my mind was fully made up. I knew the amputation was my one chance at changing my life and nothing was going to stop me. I've always been a very determined and focused person and when I get something in my sights, I make sure I go for it. It was the same with having my leg off. So while I could tell my dad didn't really want me to have it done, he was totally accepting that this was the decision I had made and I was sticking with it.

There have been certain times in my life when I've made decisions that others may have thought were wrong, or they didn't understand them, but 99 per cent of the time I've been right and I knew this was right for me. My gut, my head and my heart were all working as one: I was getting my leg amputated and there would be no going back.

I made an appointment to go and see my GP the next day. They already had the letter from my consultant in Birmingham to say that we'd discussed amputation as a possibility. When I sat down with the GP to discuss the mechanics of it, though, it was an absolutely surreal experience. It was bizarre to talk to her about phantom limb pain and the risk that I could have

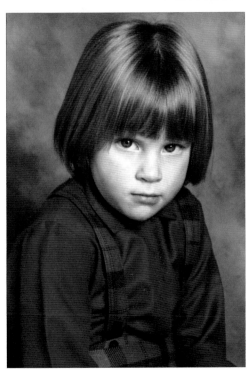

Above left: My dad Ron and mum Ann with me as a newborn.

Above right: Having a bath, aged twelve weeks.

Below left: Daddy's girl: me at the age of three.

Below right: Posing for the camera aged three.

© *Press People*

Above left: In fancy dress with my school friends, aged seven.

Above right: Ready for school with my brothers (*left to right*) Joshua, James and Hamish.

Below: Me and my brother Josh riding my aunt's horse.

© *Press People*

Top left: In my uniform as a fresh-faced recruit, aged eighteen.

Top right: Back in uniform after my amputation and hair loss.

© *Press People*

Above: In Iraq we built our own 'concrete coffins' out of breeze blocks, to protect us from mortar attacks while we were in our beds.

Image supplied by John Lewis

Left: One of the troops' accommodation blocks in Iraq.

Image supplied by John Lewis

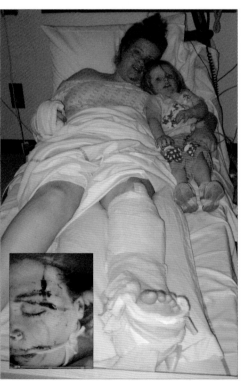

Above: The remains of the building where I was buried alive in June 2007.

Below left: Back in Birmingham directly after the blast with two-year-old Milly.

Below right: Prior to my amputation having ballooned to 21-and-a-half stone I agreed to go to a Mess event, at which Nikki played air guitar.

Inset: A glimpse of my facial injuries directly after the blast.

Above: The professional shoot in which I posed for Bryan Adams at his house, both in uniform and in a long black dress.   © *Bryan Adams*

Below: Wearing my running blade and having my photo taken with Milly, just before I completed the London Marathon.   © *John Alevroyiannis*

Above left: A smile for the camera having completed the London Marathon.

Above right: With my best friend Nikki in April 2015.

Below: On top of the world: skydiving in April 2015

Above: Enjoying motherhood again: on holiday with Milly aged nine.

Below left: Nine-year-old Milly holds her newborn sister Lexi-River.

Below right: With my miracle baby.

Above left: Swapping machine guns for spray-tan guns: me in the salon, having retrained as a beautician.

Above right: Posing for a photoshoot with newborn Lexi-River.

Below: Me and my beautiful girls at home on Lexi-River's first birthday.   © *Press People*

my leg off and none of the pain would go. This was a real fear and the first time anyone had actually mentioned it. The thought that I would go through such a big operation and still have the agony but my leg would not be there was terrifying. To have an operation like that with all the other risks attached to it and be back to square one again was almost too much to bear but although this was a very real risk, I was prepared to take a chance for my life to become better.

It was then that she said: 'We had better send you to Headley Court for a look round.' She also said she was going to request that if there were any other female soldiers in there, perhaps I could speak to them. I was delighted at the thought of speaking with another female as I had lots of questions only they'd be able to answer. My main one was: 'Would I be able to wear high heels again?'

At that time I'd not worn, never mind bought, a pair of shoes for three years. I had a space boot that I wore now and again when I wasn't in my wheelchair. I could sort of hobble around with it but it looked so awful and it was so painful that I used to take it off and just go without. Baggy, long clothes did the trick of covering my feet and I'd go barefoot in my wheelchair. I felt I couldn't show my legs as I was only able to shave one leg and then I could just go down to mid-shin on my bad leg as my foot was so deformed and in so much agony. I felt disgusting as I'd always taken so much pride in my appearance and now I couldn't.

Then there was the issue of my weight. Even if I'd been able to move around on my foot I would have struggled as I was getting out of breath even walking a few yards because I was so big. I was just trapped. I didn't feel I was a good person to be around, so I preferred to stay in on my own. My confidence was so low that I convinced myself people wouldn't like me and would want to stay away anyway. It was a vicious circle. I was making no progress whatsoever with my rehabilitation and days turned into weeks, turned into months and into years. In a cycle of doom and despair, I couldn't see anything positive at all in my life: it was just black. That's why as soon as amputation was mentioned my brain snapped out of the fog of the past three years and I thought: 'I can have my heels again, I can lose the weight and maybe even go back to work again.' For the first time since the accident I could see a glimmer of hope and a very real possibility I might have a future. The amputation gave me something positive to focus on.

So when I went back to see my consultant, Professor Porter, the following week at Birmingham hospital, my head was buzzing with positive thoughts for the future. I felt invigorated that I might be able to take control of my life once more and that I might actually be able to have a life again that wasn't one where I spent nearly 24/7 in a wheelchair at home.

By this time I'd been under Professor Porter for three years so I knew him well enough to discuss the amputation with him further. While he was at pains to stress it was not a cure-all, he said it could potentially make a difference to my life. Feeling invigorated by everything, I went back and talked with Jamie again but within forty-eight hours I was back with my GP, telling her that I wanted to go for it as soon as possible.

As part of the amputation process you must be seen by a clinical psychologist to check you are of sound mind and able to make a clear decision about having your leg amputated. A few days later, I had my appointment with her in Northern Ireland and I was champing at the bit, raring to go with everything. An impatient person at the best of times, when my mind's made up I just want to get moving with stuff. At the appointment I was a bag of nerves as I knew I was under pressure to answer her questions correctly. I felt like I was putting on a character and trying to second-guess all the things she was asking me so she would grant me the amputation. It was as if she was playing mind games with me. Of course she wasn't, she was simply doing her job, but I was so desperate to give her what I thought were the answers that she wanted to hear. I felt relief that it was over after our one-hour consultation. Shaking her hand goodbye, I just hoped that I'd done enough.

I had to wait nearly a week to see Professor Porter in Birmingham and during that time I felt sick with nerves. I could barely sleep and all I kept thinking about was the fact that this one woman stood between me and my hope of getting my life back. When I arrived for my appointment with Professor Porter I could barely get my words out and when he told me that I hadn't passed the psychological evaluation I was devastated. Any hope of starting my life again was over before it had begun. The psychologist had told him she didn't feel I was mentally ready to make the decision to have my leg off so had advised I shouldn't have it done. It was like the bottom was falling out of my world again. I'd come this far only for red tape and bureaucracy to stop me.

I could barely register his words when he then told me everything was going to be all right because while you have to have the opinion of a clinical psychologist, they do not make the final decision. He gently told me that he believed it was in my best interests to have my leg removed. And he got another doctor in as you need two consultants to override the clinical psychologist and he agreed with Professor Porter. At this I started to weep with relief. I was shaking because I couldn't believe that finally I would hopefully be free of my pain. I think because he'd been involved in my case for three years, Professor Porter had got to know me well enough to know that it was right for me. I'd tried every possible avenue to save my leg – it was something I'd so desperately wanted at the start – but it was time to move on – and that meant chopping off a leg that now only caused me pain. After all those years he was most certainly far more qualified to make the decision about my amputation than a woman I had met once for a psychological evaluation, who didn't know me and didn't know my case. I'm glad I didn't know at the evaluation she was going to say no as I don't know if I'd have been able to cope, but when Professor Porter gave it the green light I could have burst with joy.

I was then given a surgery date, there and then, and I left the hospital elated. I could barely tell Jamie as I was so emotional and relieved that this was going to happen. He just hugged me tight and told me I was doing the right thing and that he loved me and would always be there for me. I then counted down the days to the operation, which was less than three weeks away. It felt so weird to go home that night, almost a surreal anticlimax as if I could have had it done right away, I would have. Instead I had to go home and carry on life as normal despite being told I was about to have my leg chopped off!

It was so strange, I had a group of old girlfriends who came to visit me the weekend before my operation. I hadn't seen them in months as I'd just shut myself away, but I hosted a party to say goodbye to my left leg. It was the first time in so long I could have a laugh and start to feel my life was changing. I got a bit of the old Hannah back that night – it felt like the first time I'd laughed for years.

The three weeks went by in a blur and even now I didn't know what I really did. I was just so excited about having my leg off, which sounds crazy but I knew this would open the door to my future. I've got an app called Time Hop and it pulls up all your Facebook statuses from years ago, and now when I use it to look back at that time it makes me laugh as all my posts were 'Goodbye tart on two legs hello one legged wonder'! Even now it shocks me how upbeat I was about losing my limb, but I knew I had a future to look towards, instead of fear.

CHAPTER EIGHT

CAPTAIN KATE PHILP

In my heart and mind I was totally convinced that losing my leg would enable me to get my life back, so one of the most important meetings I have ever had was to happen just a week before my amputation. My surgeon, Professor Porter, as well as my military GP, whose name I sadly can't remember, was keen to find a female soldier who I could talk to about having an amputation so I would have someone with whom I could identify more than the lads. One name that kept coming up was Captain Kate Philp.

I'd never met Kate before but I knew she was, at that time, the only other serving female soldier to lose a limb in a war zone. She was only in her early thirties when she had to have her left leg amputated below the knee after the Warrior tank she was commanding ran over a hidden 50kg bomb in Afghanistan. I wanted to meet her as while I knew medically what would happen to me after my leg was removed, I wanted to ask more girly questions like: 'How do you wear heels?' and 'How do you go to the loo in the middle of the night?' All the important stuff that may seem trivial at face value but makes a massive difference in life.

Jamie and I were really lucky, as on the first day I went in for a tour of Headley Court, Captain Philp was in there as well, having a routine appointment. One of the nurses must have told her I was there because I got a message that she was up in the brew room, which is what we call the canteen, having a tea and that I should go up and join her.

The minute I sat down beside her it was like I'd known her for ages. Straight away, I started asking her all the questions I had. She laughed when I asked her about going to the loo and said: 'It's not a problem, you just hop or put your leg on!' I then bombarded her with questions, including 'Was she able to do sport?' and 'How did she feel as a woman with only one leg?' Kate was just so upbeat and positive about everything, it gave me enormous peace of mind in what I was about to do. She was different from me, in the fact she hadn't had a choice about her amputation as her leg was so terribly damaged after the blast that changed her life. She had had to have a positive outlook from day one as that was the card Fate had dealt her. While she made no bones about it not always being plain sailing, she reassured me I'd be fine.

Jamie asked her how she managed at home and did she have to take her leg off much. Another question was did she wear her leg all day, as I didn't have a clue if you were able to or if that would be too painful. It was a relief to hear she put it on in the morning and took it off at night and just went about her daily business. One of the burning questions I had, and I knew only a woman could understand this, was:

'What happens when you shave your leg?' It turned out that as you don't have a foot if you've had your leg amputated, you don't shave in a straight line from the ankle – you have to shave the whole circumference of your leg where the limb has been removed. She also told me a lot about the potential skin infections I could get from shaving. Women can get lumps and bumps anyway from shaving through ingrown hairs, but imagine wrapping that hair in a lump of airless silicone and you get the drift of how bad it could be. It didn't put me off, though – there was no way I was going to have hairy legs on top of everything else! Her overriding message was: 'Well, I've only got one leg now so I'll just have to get on with it'. She was living her life and what I took from the meeting was confirmation I'd be able to get on with mine again.

I was exceptionally at ease with what was about to happen as the amputation, although necessary, was being done after I'd had a chance to grieve for my leg. For three agonising years I'd suffered hell, so it was a relief to be breaking free from it. For that, I feel very fortunate for it was a fresh start, not a terrible, devastating shock.

The closer it got to the amputation day, the calmer I seemed to get about what was a massive, life-changing procedure. I'd had so many different operations at that point I almost felt my body was invincible, and I'd become fairly complacent about having surgery because I was so used to it. The fact that I was grossly overweight and that this could hamper both the surgery and its effects didn't really come into my head.

The most important thing I did in those short weeks leading up to the surgery was to tell Milly that Mummy was going to have her leg removed. I hadn't a clue where to start so one evening I went on my laptop and googled 'How do you tell a child you are having an amputation' and it came as a surprise to me that there wasn't actually anything at that time in any of the search engines. 'How the hell am I going to tell her?' I wondered. Jamie and I sat down, discussed it and decided I would get some pictures of women wearing prosthetic legs that I could print off from the Internet. I wanted them to be as positive as possible so I made sure that I got a few of female athletes wearing blades and women wearing a prosthetic with a high heel. It was important to me that I show her positive things so I could tell her that Mum was going to be like these women and have my bad leg taken off and a brilliant new leg put on.

She was five by then, so I took the time to explain it all to her and she just sat there, not uttering a word and taking it all in. She'd grown up with a mum who was severely disabled and in all honesty, our relationship was very badly damaged because of this as I'd become an absentee mother who was living in the same house as her. Even now, looking back, I can barely admit to myself that there wasn't much of a bond between us at that point in my life due to what had happened to me. I'd been away and out of her life more than I'd been with her as I was away in Iraq and then in and out of hospital. I think it was hard for Milly to comprehend properly what was going on in as she was just so used to me not being there, so I think she just thought of my amputation as 'Mummy's going to hospital again'. Back then I felt so distant from her, which is a horrific thing to feel about your own child. Now, even all these years later, I feel great sadness if I think back to that time and our relationship. I just felt so cheated. I'd missed out on so much of her childhood due to my injury.

So when I told her, for the first time since the blast that I actually felt hopeful and having my leg off would mean I was going to get better, I inwardly hoped that would mean our relationship as much as my leg. I just hugged her tight and a tear rolled down my cheek as I whispered to her, 'I love you and I'm going to be a better mum to you now.' I knew I'd be able to do more with her and actually give her a childhood that included me. It breaks my heart even now to think that I was so injured it had got to that and I doubted myself as a mother. Telling her that night was one of the biggest moments of my life as it meant I was finally going to get to know her and do the things 'normal' mums did. I wanted to make her proud of me and I was determined that the amputation and my life moving forward was going to transform everything for us both. She just hugged me back and smiled and that meant more to me than anything else in the world. It confirmed once again (though I didn't need reminding) that the amputation was the right thing for me.

Despite that, moments of dread did start to creep in as the clocked ticked ever nearer to my op. I don't know if it's because telling Milly made the whole thing seem more real to me, but it seemed to activate a little voice in my head that said not only was this serious, it could be an operation that I didn't come back from.

One evening, when Jamie was at work and Milly was safely tucked up in bed, I decided to do something I had only done once before and that was to write a letter that was to be opened up at my funeral if I didn't pull through the operation. It was so different from the letter I'd written before I went to war. Back then I was a fresh-faced new mum with all my life in front of me. Now, just three years later, I knew how things could change in the blink of an eye and that no one is invincible and no one lives forever.

I was trembling when I got the pen and paper out and sat at the kitchen table but it was something I wanted and needed to get down in black and white. I started off by telling everyone how much I loved them, and that if I died I wanted Jamie to move on and find happiness with someone else. He was – and is – such a wonderful man he deserves to be happy in life. The only thing I asked was if another woman was in Milly's life that she didn't call her Mum because that's the title I wanted to maintain. When I saw Milly's name down on the sheet of paper that's when the tears flowed. The thought that I might never see my little beautiful baby girl again was too much, but I knew I wasn't being a proper mum to her so I had to go through with the amputation. I also wrote that they would always be financially looked after and that my parents must always have full access to Milly. Not that I felt this needed to be spelt out, but in my head I wanted to get my affairs in order so I knew if the worst was to happen I had left instructions about my final wishes. I don't know what drove me to decide to write the letter but it ended up being two sides of A4 paper. I've still got it sealed in a safe place in my house and I've never opened it. It may be silly superstition but I feel like I never want to open it as if I do then I'm tempting fate and who knows what would happen?

I was so anxious as I wrote the letter, I clenched up inside. It was only once I'd got it all down and licked the envelope firmly shut that I felt I could breathe again. I'd been given a self-meditation and breathing cassette by the hospital to try and keep my anxiety under control, so to clear my head, I decided to put it on. You focus on bits of your body and tense them and relax them from your feet up while breathing deeply and calmly. I lay there alone in bed, listening to the tape. When it got to the bit where it said 'and now relax your left leg and your left foot' I thought: 'This is the last time I'm going to do this at home and this is the last time I'm going to have my leg here.'

Lying there alone in the dark with just the tape for company I got a strange sense of calm. This was it – I was saying goodbye to my leg for the final time. I count myself so lucky for moments like those as unlike some of the other guys at Headley Court, I didn't wake up to my leg being missing. Instead I had time to say goodbye to it, as if it was a bereavement, but at the same time I felt I'd grieved enough and now it was time to say goodbye to it forever.

I was admitted to the hospital two days before my operation. Prior to being admitted I felt that Milly needed a holiday and a hospital was no place for a five-year-old, so Mum had agreed that she could stay with her in Cumbria. That allowed me to get some head space, with no distractions, to mentally prepare myself for the op. We agreed they'd all come down to see me post-op before taking her on holiday to Whitby and then placing her in our village primary school in Cumbria for a few months while I recuperated.

I'd barely slept a wink the night before my admission due to nervous excitement – I just wanted to crack on and have it done. Yet, at the same time, the reality of what I was doing had firmly sunk in. I don't remember anything at all I said to Jamie on the way to the hospital. Putting my bag of clothes in the back of the car was the last concrete memory and then I was lost in my own thoughts until we pulled up right outside the main entrance. My mind was in overdrive, flooded by thoughts and sheer terror at what I was about to do. I kept thinking of Milly, my family, the fact that I would have one less limb. It was a jumbled-up mess, which I realise was probably due to extreme anxiety and the enormity of what I was about to do. There would be no going back from this and while I was ready, it was still terrifying.

The one thing I do remember asking Jamie repeatedly was would he still find me attractive with one leg? He kept reassuring me that he would but I wasn't even listening to him. I just kept asking and asking him. I still felt hope in my heart and I knew I was doing the right thing but the minute we entered the hospital the real terror began. I was on my crutches as we walked across the foyer to check in and my head started to spin. Sick to the pit of my stomach, I started to shake with fear. There was no going back, but that didn't make it any easier.

On the day of my operation, right from the start things didn't go well. I had to have an epidural beforehand, which helps your brain forget the pain. The theory is that after you've had the amputation there will be no phantom limb pain as once you are put to sleep, the body will have no memory of you ever having experienced any pain where the amputation takes place, as you never felt it happen.

In reality, having the epidural was a nightmare as the doctor involved had trouble finding a place to put it in. I blame this on me being so grossly overweight that they just couldn't get the right space on my spine. This meant the numbness worked on some parts of my body but not on others. I knew my twenty-one and a half stones would be a problem for the operation but I never expected it to hamper it this much before we'd even got off the starting blocks. The doctor concerned had to repeatedly administer the epidural but it just wouldn't work in the way that it should have done.

I then had to just sit there for forty-five minutes being monitored before I went down to Theatre. During that time Jamie spoke to me to calm my nerves. It was the first time I thought: 'Oh God, what if something goes wrong and I can't see Milly again?' That time was awful and an absolute eternity. Thoughts raced through my mind. I was truly terrified about what I was about to do and what was going to happen to me. Jamie walked by my side, holding my hand as they took me down to Theatre. Ashen-faced, he looked more scared than me and I thought I could see tears in his eyes. Before saying he'd see me in a few hours he hugged me tight and told me everything was going to be alright and how much he loved me and couldn't wait to see me after the surgery. We kissed and then I was taken through some doors on my trolley into Theatre.

I tried focusing on the strip lighting to control my fear. All I could think about was Milly and Jamie and how I couldn't wait to hold both of them in my arms again. I was then given an injection to put me to sleep. Mr Porter squeezed my shoulder and said, 'Don't worry, Hannah. Everything is going to be OK.' Then I was asked to count down from ten and when I got to eight everything went black.

The next, fleeting, memory I have is of waking up in bed and screaming in agony. The pain from where my leg had gone was like nothing I had ever felt before. Then I was instantly knocked out again. I found out later from one of the nurses the epidural hadn't worked properly and that's why I was in agony, and so they had to knock me out again straight away to try and stop my pain.

Sometime later I woke up again to find myself on the ward. The curtains were pulled round my bed and immediately I started trying to feel for my leg, which wasn't there. I was on a huge amount of pain medication and I remember I kept reaching for my stump. Jamie was sat waiting for me with this massive grin on his face and a huge bunch of flowers. He just embraced me and told me he was so proud and how much he loved me. The first thing I asked was whether Milly was OK. He told me she was doing great and blissfully happy with my parents and none the wiser about what was going on. This was the first time in days that I actually felt I was beginning to relax for I knew Jamie and our beautiful daughter were fine and I'd come through the operation. Then Mum and Dad came in with Milly and my brothers. I was so pleased to see them. The job was done and now I could start focusing on the future and our life together.

Within a day I could push myself using my arms off my hospital trolley onto my bed. My family spent every minute of visiting hours by my bedside. Dad was messing around in my wheelchair and then taking lungfuls from my oxygen canister and we were laughing and joking. There was just a palpable sense of relief.

On the second day I had a surprise visitor: Kate Philp. It was such a kind gesture from her and a brilliant surprise for me. She brought me a plant for my room, some chocolate brownies and some fruit, as she knew how terrible the canteen could be in there. She was just so happy for me and we chatted about how I was feeling and how well the operation seemed to have gone. It was a morale boost and I was so thankful that she took the time to come there just to see me. But while she was visiting me I remember saying to her: 'Kate, it's so weird but at times I can't get my breath.' At that point it was only now and then so I was actually laughing about it, as I didn't think it was serious. I wasn't in any pain at this point because I was so doped up. I was taking a lot of drugs so I wasn't quite with it; I thought it was odd but didn't make a big deal. And to be honest, Kate's visit was a massive diversion as it gave me a real boost.

But after she left I began to feel quite unwell and I started to intermittently gasp for air. At first the doctors thought I was coming down with flu. Mum came to see me, with Dad and my brothers, before she headed north with Milly. They had brought me a Nintendo DS game so I had something to amuse myself with when I was recuperating, but while I remember seeing their faces, I don't recall anything else of the meeting. I didn't know it then but my brain wasn't getting enough oxygen for it to be actually making any memories. Mum seemed to have a sixth sense: she became really worried about me; she just felt something was not quite right and she didn't want to leave me, but I insisted it was the right thing for Milly. I kissed her goodbye and repeated that this was no place for such a small child.

By the time Jamie arrived for visiting hours my chest had started to get really tight and I began wheezing quite badly. I phoned Mum several times as I started to feel worse and worse, and she told me to keep her in touch with what was happening. First, they moved me from a side room to be nearer the nurses' station so they could keep a closer eye on me. Immediately, I rang Mum to tell her and she became more concerned than I've ever heard her sound. I said: 'I'm just ringing, Mum, to tell you that I love you.' I always seem to do that in a crisis – I just wanted to speak to my mum and let her know I love her and to hear that she loved me.

Later, when my breathing started to become laboured and

I began panting, the doctors became increasingly concerned. I tried talking to Jamie but I was really struggling for breath and not making any sense whatsoever. Words were coming out of my mouth but they were all jumbled and slurred. He was concerned, but at first everyone thought with some intravenous antibiotics it would pass. Later, after visiting hours I continued to deteriorate until one of the doctors told me: 'We are going to move you to Intensive Care, just to help with your breathing.'

That's the last conscious memory I have before slipping into a coma.

CHAPTER NINE

COMA

Even now, Jamie says it was one of the worst moments of his life. It was shortly after 11pm on 1 June 2010 and he'd just settled down to sleep when he got a knock on the door of the special family room he was staying in at the hospital. A nurse told him he needed to get over to the ward right away as I had type 2 respiratory failure and sepsis, a condition that was causing all the organs in my body to slowly shut down. Jamie immediately knew how serious it was. He has told me since then that he ran over to the ward without even shutting the door, following the medical officer. It was clear I was dying and he knew he had to get to me.

In the short space of time before he got there I had been put in a medically induced coma and still he was not allowed to see me. At the time they were working on me to try and do everything possible to save me. He just had to sit on his own in the relatives' room anxiously waiting for any news. I was so ill I wasn't even moved to Intensive Care at that point as it was deemed too risky. Within hours I was transferred there on full life support with a machine breathing for me. It was absolutely horrific as we'd gone through so much and for this to happen, on top of everything else, was too cruel to bear.

With any kind of surgery there are always risks but I was just one of the few very unlucky people who developed a complication. I blame my weight, as the heavier you are when you have major surgery, the likelihood of complications increases. But doctors have since told me I was just very, very unlucky. I never breathed deeply after I came round from the surgery and I think this made my lungs sticky and then I got pneumonia. This infection led to sepsis and my immune system was so weakened that my organs went into full failure almost straight away. It was a domino effect and the doctors feared I might not make it.

Knowing Mum and Dad must be exhausted from the drive north, it wasn't until the following morning that Jamie broke the news. Mum had only arrived in Whitby a matter of hours earlier, but she immediately said: 'If Hannah's in Intensive Care and there's any chance at all that she's going to die, then she's going to die with her family around her.' She dropped Milly off with my aunty, who lived in the town, and immediately drove south again, picking up Dad en route. They arrived by my bedside at 8.30pm, long after visiting hours, and were taken into a side room with a big box of tissues on the table and given a cup of tea. The doctor explained I'd developed an infection, they didn't know what it was and they were growing cultures to try and find out.

Mum asked: 'Is Hannah going to die?'

'Yes, she could do,' the doctor admitted. She explained that without the respirator I would have already died as the infection was causing too much carbon dioxide and not enough oxygen. I was young, strong and fit, which was in my favour, but my weight was against my recovery and could also have been a contributing factor to what was happening.

When Mum came to my bedside she says it wasn't me lying there – it was like a shell of me with nothing else there at all. She touched me and there was no response; a respirator was breathing for me, my cheeks were flushed and I was hot to touch. There were six syringe drivers pumping a cocktail of drugs and antibiotics into me, countless beeping machines and two dedicated nurses working on me all the time. Heartbreakingly, there was no response when she spoke to me. Nothing at all, not even a curling of the fingers. Where my leg should have been the sheet of the bed was just flat, smooth and untouched. But no one worried about that, they just wanted me back.

Each day of my coma was monotonous. Only two visitors were allowed at a time, so everyone took it in turns so there was always someone with me during visiting hours. Mum would come first thing, ring a bell for access to Critical Care and then wait in a side room for the nurse to come and collect her once I was ready. Once they sat beside me, they talked to me. In Intensive Care at the time there were lots of other Army injured, including a number of Gurkhas, and their parents would be doing the same, so there was a quiet hum of voices in the ward.

The nurses did everything for me and the other desperately ill patients. They combed my hair, shaved the men who were also in the ward, and all my bodily functions were taken care of with various tubes. Mum would watch families arriving each day, including the Gurkha mums, who would always arrive in brightly coloured dresses and were often accompanied by a member of their regiment to support and translate. Mum wondered what they must have thought, coming from a different culture to see their son horrifically injured in Intensive Care.

Initially, I was in a bay by myself, but then some poor soul was put in the bed next to me while I was in the coma and died. The Army moved Mum, Dad and Jamie into a nearby hotel as in all honesty they probably thought I was going to follow closely behind so they wanted to make them as comfortable as possible as the levels of stress they were experiencing were horrendous. I'm just so thankful Milly wasn't there to see me during this period. She was so little she wouldn't have understood what was going on and it would have been an awful environment for her to be in.

By day three I'd become swollen. My wedding ring became tight and I was put on dialysis to try and cool my blood as my temperature raged. The doctor agreed there was a small improvement but I wasn't out of the woods as I'd developed pneumonia in my left lung.

Five days in there was the first sign of hope. The consultant came in and told Mum and Dad she was 'cautiously optimistic' and that the levels of infection were improving. My dialysis machine was removed but the ventilator remained. During Mum and Dad's visiting time I began to move my hand and chew on the tubes in my mouth. Dad immediately rang Jamie, who rushed to my bedside. Later in the afternoon, while my bed was being changed, I began to move my head and legs, initially waving my arms a little, but then I became agitated. Apparently everyone was calling my name, desperately trying to get me to surface. I began to respond to Mum's voice and apparently each time she spoke to me I'd open my eyes, but they were glazed and unfocused. Clearly on some level I was registering she was there and speaking to me. I know this because Mum kept a diary for the entire ten days. One of the medical staff suggested to her it might be a way of coping with what was going on and trying to get her head around the fact that her only daughter, me, was fighting again with all her strength to live. She also hoped I'd be able to read it if I recovered and wanted me to know what had happened during my lost days, not only to me, but also Milly.

I have read the diary but only once as it was so painful to read. It made me realise just how difficult it was for everyone around me, particularly being a mother myself. My aunt was also good at texting photos of Milly, including her with the school's newborn chicks, which she was able to show Jamie. It was a relief to find out she had been having a fantastic time with our extended family and her life hadn't been touched by the horror of what was going on.

There was a special area of the hospital which military families could use, where Mum chatted to the other parents, who all supported each other. You could go over there, make cups of tea, cook a meal and also do your laundry; staff were constantly there to provide help and support, too. You'd ring a bell to go in, give the name of the Military casualty and a member of staff would let you in with a smile, asking, 'Would you like to talk or is there anything we can do to help?'

Initially my dad had asked the doctor: 'What can we do to help?' The answer was simple: 'Support each other.' So when visiting times ended, they did all sorts of things to distract from the stress: visit an art gallery, have a picnic in the park or even taking a walk. An activity was planned for every day.

Later, when they'd come back, they'd tell me what they'd been doing, trying to coax me from my coma. At times Mum admits she almost enjoyed her afternoons out, but hidden underneath the laughter was the knowledge that I was lifeless, back at the hospital.

On day six it was a case of two steps forward, three steps back. In the morning I obeyed an instruction from a nurse to squeeze her hand, then I began to move when I coughed, pulling faces, chewing on my tube and flailing my arms about in the air. It was distressing, but the doctors tried to reassure everyone that it was perfectly normal. The consultant explained that there is a Glasgow Scale for a depth of coma and I had been at three, which was the deepest.

While all this was going on in the real world I was living another life in my coma. This sounds absolutely surreal but they say that the mind is capable of many incredible things and very little is actually fully understood. After what I experienced I believe this. I vividly remember starting my life again: in my mind I watched myself being born, growing up, getting married and having lots of kids. It was like the most vivid and brightest dream ever and I was starring in it like a home movie of a life I'd never had. I remember being aware I was dying in my dream world and accepting it.

While I was in this state, doctors had decided that I would benefit from an experimental drug designed to make the veins more elastic in order to improve blood flow around my body. They needed my family's consent, prepared to grasp any glimmer of light in what was an awful, pitch-black situation. The drug worked by making your arteries and veins more elastic and cutting down the strain on your body. This in turn helped the body to heal itself. The doctors explained to Mum,

Dad and Jamie that the Military, as a matter of course, never allowed experimental drugs to be used on soldiers so the decision had to be made as a family unit. Between them they all agreed I should have it: they just wanted me back and any chance of achieving that was a chance worth taking. The drug was administered straight away and it may well have saved my life.

The first sign that things were improving was when the machinery around me began to be removed. First, the breathing machinery, then the syringe drivers began to reduce in number. Mum had learned the signs to look for before they went back to the wards. Although I wasn't totally out of the woods yet, things were looking more optimistic and it seemed I had turned a corner. When I began to wake from the coma the first thing I did was attempt to smile at Mum, although it apparently looked more like a rictus grimace when she mentioned Milly. My throat was so sore from the machines and sometimes I managed forty-one breaths a minute, other times just sixteen. I only know this as medical staff told my mum and she told me later; at the time I was very confused, drifting in and out of consciousness.

At one point I told everyone to 'shut up' and I seem to have believed I'd been sectioned; I was totally unaware that the white walls were those of a hospital room. But my first real memory is of people washing me and I remember feeling irritable and trying to roll to get away from them – I just wanted to be left alone. I remember my mum and Jamie leaning over me in bed and saying to me: 'Hannah, you've been in a coma.'

I was so disorientated that I started to get really cross with them. 'No, I haven't! What the hell are you talking about?' I slurred angrily. I was just so cross, I thought everyone was lying to me. All my Mum and Jamie wanted to do was kiss and hug me but I was having none of it. I was so disorientated that I barely knew my own name. Although I was rude to Mum my main rage was directed at Jamie. I told him: 'Get me out of here now!' and 'Go and get the car and park outside and drive me home!' The irony of the whole situation was I could barely move, let alone walk, as my body was so weak and all my muscles had wasted away after spending ten days in a coma. I had so little strength I couldn't actually lift my own hand up to my face. In fact I was so poorly for the two days after the op that I had to get people to scratch my face if I had an itch and even blow my nose for me.

I finally came round fully after ten days and my behaviour was totally inappropriate and very strange. It was as if all my natural social graces had gone. No one was sure if I was ever going to be Hannah again; I was just saying weird things. Even though my mum kept saying to me: 'Hannah, you are in Intensive Care', I thought I had been on holiday on a cruise. I insisted that my huge yacht had been bobbing and that I was feeling seasick. On one occasion I called a consultant over as I decided I wanted to get up even though I was still attached to goodness knows what. I issued an imperious order: 'Just run along over there and do you see that wheelchair? Can you bring it over here for me.' It was someone else's wheelchair firstly. And secondly, you don't speak to a consultant like that! He took it terribly well. I suppose he must have been used to this sort of thing, although Mum apologised profusely for my behaviour. Why I thought I'd appropriate someone else's wheelchair is beyond me!

I flirted shamelessly with anyone, whether it was a nurse, doctor or another patient – it was as if all my inner filters and good manners had been switched off. Loads of crazy things came out of my mouth. One nurse was asked: 'Why did I have no toes on my other foot?' He replied: 'You do have toes.' I then told Dad I had a fancy chair that goes up and down stairs (referring to my trolley wheels) and I begged them to tell everyone I was not a looney. Perhaps the most poignant thing I said was: 'I can't sleep. I'm frightened if I sleep, it will happen again.' All the while Mum continued to log everything in the diary – while they'd been warned this might happen, it didn't ease the shock, though.

On the second day I told Mum: 'It was really busy in here last night. They were stacking the stretchers one on top of another. There have been loads of casualties.' Mum later told me she looked over at one of the doctors, who discretely shook his head. It was just another bizarre hallucination. Another time I was also obsessed with dead bodies being stacked up by my bed – which of course also hadn't happened. I told my dad I wasn't able to sleep because I'd been on an aeroplane all night. When he gently tried to correct me and tell me there was no aeroplane, I told him to get out of my sight and get out of my room, so he had to leave. I was genuinely slightly mad. And because people gently tried to pull me back to reality I became convinced everyone was having me on and they were all conspiring against me. The fact is my mind was so muddled from the coma and what I'd been through it wasn't making any sense of anything.

At one point, as I was becoming more lucid, the hospital arranged for a physiotherapist to come and see me. A nurse said: 'Do you want to have a wash before he comes?' Just the thought of feeling clean again at that moment was heavenly. All my armpit hair had grown, my hair was matted and my legs were covered in thick hair as well. She gave me a full bed bath, taking about an hour. And she did everything for me: shaved my armpits, gently washed my scalp. On the one hand it was so degrading but on another I simply didn't care as I just wanted to feel human again. I was still being fed through a tube, so I had a rectal tube fitted as well – basically the food was going in a tube at one end and coming out of a tube at the other. And so the nurses decided to remove that before I saw the physiotherapist just to make it more comfortable for me.

When the physiotherapist did show up he pulled back the curtains around my bed and I saw a young, attractive bloke. My heart sank. 'Right, Hannah, we're going to get you standing up,' he said (he had a walking frame with him). He then started to help me get out of the bed with one of the nurses. The effort of standing up was monumental. Every single cell in my body was screaming in agony but I was determined to get upright. The worst thing was I had only been standing for a split second when unfortunately nature took its course and I actually had an accident and soiled myself on the hospital floor. My face was scarlet.

I thought: 'Oh, my God, I've just stood up for the first time, which is amazing, but I've shat myself in the process and in front of a man!' Thankfully he left the room and the nurses cleaned up the floor and me. I just kept saying, 'Oh, my God, I can't believe I've done that! I'm so sorry.' There was a part of me that knew I would be able to laugh about it at some point in my life but I also knew it wouldn't be for quite a while. He had another go about an hour later and it was the most effort I've ever made in my life to stand upright again. Consequently, lightning struck twice! I was so mortified, I shouted at him, begging him: 'Don't ever come back and see me ever again!' – and he didn't. He actually fled the room. I must have terrified him. The whole thing was just awful; you lose your pride and your dignity. I was so grateful to the medical staff and people around me and now I know it didn't really matter.

Thank God the hallucinations and crazy behaviour only lasted for three days. Although my family had been warned that this would happen, they were understandably anxious they weren't going to get me back. Four days later I was moved on to the main military ward and because I was the only female, I was given a side room so I had a bit more privacy. I also had a special 'floating' airbed to stop me getting bed sores. The remote control was a bit dicky but it's the most uncomfortable bed I've ever slept on.

As a result of my coma my face had swollen up, pushing my eyes slightly out of their sockets. My lips were huge, swollen and covered in sores. I was unrecognisable. When I saw my appearance I gasped. I looked like an alien with these bug-like eyes and hugely swollen lips and cheeks. The back of my hands were so swollen they looked like they had half-tennis balls under the skin. My body was literally double its size due to the build up of fluid because I'd been in the coma for so long it hadn't had a chance to move anywhere.

Mum and Dad spoke to one of the doctors and asked if I was going to look like that forever. He said, 'Look like what?' So they showed him a picture of me from a holiday a few years previously. It was like two different people. Thankfully, he assured them it would go within a few weeks.

As the days passed, the main ward was like a breath of fresh air. It was as if I was rejoining life again. People popped in and out of my room all the time and my recovery was fast.

I felt invigorated and despite being in pain I was excited and just so thankful to still be alive. From then on I started getting physio every day and was taught how to get in and out of my wheelchair as I hadn't had my prosthetics fitted yet due to all the trauma of the coma. Every hour I felt a little stronger and more positive; I felt I could do anything. I don't know where it came from in my brain but I started thinking to myself: 'I've got rid of that leg now, I'm going to be able to run again.' I hadn't even got out of my hospital bed yet but I felt the world was full of possibilities instead of dead ends.

'What can I do that's a really big challenge?' I thought, for I needed a goal. And then I decided: 'I know, I'm going to run the London Marathon.' I loved watching it on TV every year and so I decided to do it for the charity Blesma: The British Limbless Ex-Service Men's Association, an amazing national charity who support servicemen and women when they have lost limbs. Their representatives had come to visit me in my hospital bed. The charity has loads of activities to encourage the limbless to lead normal lives, including skiing, scuba diving, ski-bob and horse-riding. Nothing is off-limits. They also advise and help ex-military with anything from adapting their homes to which benefits they are eligible for, as well as giving guidance and advice for the rest of your life.

So when everyone was around my bed during that evening's visiting time I said: 'Hang on, I've got something to tell you all.' It was my mum, dad, Milly and Jamie, who all immediately went quiet. And then I announced: 'I'm going to do the London Marathon in 2012!' They just said: 'Yeah, alright.' I'd been hallucinating so I think at first they thought it was just another thing I was saying under the influence of drugs.

A week after I'd come out of the coma my best friend Nikki

was allowed to be the first non-family member to come in and see me. I had expected her to be shocked when she saw me. The first thing out of her mouth was, 'Oh God, Hannah, you haven't shaved your legs! I can't have you sitting here with hairy legs!' Only Nikki could say something like that after everything I'd been through. It made me burst out laughing – it was actually the first time I'd laughed and felt like the old me. She got a little bowl from one of the nurses, some soap and a Bic razor and set to work. My stump had actually healed brilliantly as I had been in the coma for so long it had been rested. She shaved my right leg, no problem but obviously I didn't have part of my left leg anymore, so she shaved all down the bit of leg I did have and when she got to my stump, which still had staples in it at this point, she carefully went round each one. Nikki is so squeamish normally, but it was such an incredibly kind, loving gesture that even now I don't think I can tell her how much that meant to me at that moment in my life.

Then, after she'd done that, one of the nurses came into the room and said: 'We're going to remove all your staples now.' Nikki held my hand throughout the whole thing. It was a massive moment for me as it was the first time I'd seen my leg properly hair-free and without any of the ugly staples in it. I was so glad Nikki was there with me. But I looked down at it and thought: 'Right, this is me. This is how it is now and I'm cracking on with life and I'm going to squeeze every last opportunity out of it!' I had tears in my eyes: I was so happy I'd been given another chance at life and I was grabbing it. As we sat talking I said to her: 'Do you know what Nikki?' I think I need a girly holiday after all of this. And she said: 'Well, why don't we book somewhere? Where do you want to go?' and I immediately said: 'I've always wanted to go to the Bahamas.' So there and then we said we'd do it.

I knew everything would be OK and I was going to see Milly again shortly. We had made a conscious decision as a family not to tell her about the coma as I didn't want her to be scared about anything. Even now, years later, she still doesn't know anything about it; I just wanted to protect her, like any mother would. Today I'm at peace with the fact she's going to find out and I've decided to give her a copy of this book, with a personal message inside the cover, to she can read my story for herself and share it at Show And Tell at school. Because I'm not that sick shadow of my former self anymore, This is something that happened to me in her past, whereas back then, it was something we were living through.

Nikki picked me up on discharge day from the hospital. Normally I would have gone straight to Headley Court for rehabilitation. Because I'd been so ill, I had to go home to my parents' house in Cumbria for a few weeks of recuperation first while Jamie packed up the house in Ireland, ready to move back to the UK. He was transferred to the Royal Electrical Mechanical Engineers, who are an amazing unit, while I was transferred to the Army's long-term sick list, so I was no longer attached to a unit. But it meant I would get all the help I needed to set me on the road to recovery. I'm impatient and it was annoying as I wanted to start straight away at Headley, but I was just thankful I was alive. The Army had arranged transport to take me to my parents. Milly would be there as well and I couldn't wait to see her.

One of the physio team wasn't happy about me going home as they were concerned about how I would cope with one leg. What they didn't seem to register was I'd been coping with only one leg for years as my foot had been so damaged I couldn't use the leg anyway. This meant I knew how to move my body to get up and down stairs, how to use the toilet and have a bath. I had such trouble convincing them, but I just fought them every step of the way so I could get home and see Milly. I had to show them I could do necessities like getting in and out of a bath and in and out of bed. They told me not to go up and down stairs as they were worried I'd hurt myself, so I lied, omitting to tell them my parents' former watermill is three storeys high, and said I was going to sleep in my parents' lounge on their ground floor. In my mind as I was agreeing to it I was thinking: 'There's not a hope in hell's chance that is happening! I will be sleeping on the top floor, in my old bedroom, like a normal person.'

The first thing I did when I arrived at my mum's was to crawl up two flights of stairs just to prove to myself I could do it. Even though I was still exhausted from the coma, I had no pain at all from the amputation. It was the first time in years I was free from the burden of my damaged leg and I felt incredible – it was like I was throwing off the chains of my former life. That is the only thing I've got the coma to thank for, as I was unconscious for the period when I would have been suffering from phantom limb pain. Even now I don't really get it. What I do sometimes experience is a feeling like little electrodes of pain tingling in my lower limb where my leg used to be.

My heart nearly burst with joy when Milly came home from school and flung her arms around me in my wheelchair, excitedly screaming: 'Mummy!' I just held her so tight and cried with happiness. Then I told her: 'Mummy will never leave you again.' She then looked at my leg and shook it like a handshake, as if it was the most normal thing in the world. 'Hello, Twinkle,' she said when she did it. I don't know where the name came from, but that's what she called my stump and the name's stuck.

Then that was it as far as Milly was concerned. Mummy was back with one leg and Twinkle the stump, and that's how life was. It's never been a big deal and it still isn't. That night, Milly slept with me in bed and it was wonderful to be able to cuddle her. The next few weeks were great! My mum and dad were amazing. Jamie flew over as regularly as he could from Ireland while he continued to work and arrange to move house back to the UK.

Every day I was getting my strength back, I was spending time with Milly, playing with her and reading her bedtime stories. It was like my life was finally coming together. I couldn't wait to get to Headley Court as I knew that was when I was going to transform myself forever.

The second day after my hospital discharge I rang Blesma and said: 'Please can I have one of your spaces, I want to run in the London Marathon. Actually, please can I have two as I want somebody to run with me because I've only just lost my leg and if I get stuck, they are going to push me in my wheelchair.'

The woman on the phone was lovely. She said: 'How far down the line are you?'

'Just a few weeks,' I replied. 'I haven't even got my first prosthetic leg yet.'

Even she was surprised, but she said, 'OK.' She knew it was achievable as they work with amputees.

That night I announced to my family: 'I've confirmed my two places in the London Marathon next year.' Even then they were a bit disbelieving but I just quietly got on with it and I knew with the help I was going to get at Headley Court, I had a fighting chance of completing it. The irony was I didn't even particularly love running – I ran because I had to as I was in the Army and it was a part of Army life. But I also wanted to prove to my family I wasn't hallucinating when I said I'd do the marathon. I was determined to do it and I knew I would.

'Just you watch me!' I thought.

CHAPTER TEN

HEADLEY
COURT

Being at Headley Court in the summer of 2010, shortly before the anniversary of my blast, was like going back to my first days of early training. It was a chance for me to mentally and physically immerse myself in a place I knew and loved. Even when it was tough, I relished every second of it. I knew it was the beginning of me getting my life back. Equally important was the fact I became one of the lads again. It was just like old times and although I was a novelty, as the only girl, it was great to be part of a gang again.

Even though Captain Kate Philp had been there before to recuperate with her injuries, she was an officer. As I was just a normal soldier I had the same status as most of the lads, which in my mind meant I belonged. The other guys there at the same time as me were so supportive. Finally, I felt I had people to communicate with who truly knew what I was feeling. When I was in the gym they'd push me to work hard to keep up with them. During all my physio sessions, if they did an hour of weights then I'd do an hour, too. There was no way I was going to let anyone, male or female, get the better of me! The effect it had on me was brilliant and for the first time in years I felt like I was in control of my own body, not the other way around, and I was fast making progress.

Headley Court is run day-to-day very much like the Army. They take a roll call every morning at 8.30am after breakfast and you have to be there, no excuses. Initially, I had six months rehabilitation on a rotation of three weeks on and three weeks off, with weekends at home. Inside, there's a fully functioning hospital; I was put in a room there for the first six months but because I was coming and going I didn't have a chance to add any homely touches, although I always put a photo of Milly next to my bed. I was supplied with a wheelchair and I was taught to use it. Around Headley Court, everywhere had been adapted for wheelchair users – wider doors, big bathrooms and lift buttons you could reach easily. When I first arrived I was already used to seeing people with single amputations and even double amputees, so I didn't bat an eyelid even though there were quite a few of them. I was shocked at first, though, when a young man walked in who was a triple amputee. But I couldn't help but be inspired by him as he strolled into the room as it made me determined – if he could do it, I could too. You saw all sorts of injuries at Headley Court, so after being there that first time there wasn't anything that could shock me. Rather I was in awe of the men's determination to achieve and recover despite often devastating injuries.

While I was desperate to get walking on my prosthetic, first I had to master my wheelchair as I couldn't go out until the occupational therapist was confident I could manage alone, but the rehab was so intensive that at first I was too exhausted to go out anyway. Once they were happy I was competent, I was downgraded to standard living accommodation: a room adapted for wheelchair users with an en suite shower. There was a single bed with a view out over the grounds. Decorated in standard military magnolia, it was no-frills and functional. I didn't even unpack my suitcase when I was there – I spent all the time I could concentrating on my rehab.

The food was amazing at Headley Court. It was tailored to help those who had gained weight after they'd become sedentary due to injury: there was a salad bar, fresh sandwiches made to order and low-calorie hot food. In addition to the healthy options there were chips and comfort food for the die-hards. Compared to standard Army fare, it was amazing!

Every day, everyone has to head to the gym, no matter what their disability. Anyone from a triple amputee to someone with a brain injury must push themselves to the limit. It didn't matter what was wrong with you, you just had to get on with it, doing things like weights to music, which was led by an instructor at the front of the gym. If you're a triple amputee and you can't pick up the weights they are using, you are just given another set – there is absolutely no exception made for you whatsoever. While it may sound harsh, it is that lack of compromise that gets people motivated. That attitude was one of the main things that kept me going in there and which has kept me going since. Quite simply, you don't have time to moan or dwell on what's happened to you; you just have to crack on and deal with it.

Obviously, while my condition was serious, there were other people in there who were far worse off than me. Seeing them do well in physical exercise made me think, 'Well, if they can do it, I can do it, too.'

You do an hour's exercise in the morning then you are allocated a personal instructor, with whom you do one-to-one physical training for the rest of the day. That involves something low-key like stretching to something much more strenuous such as wheelchair boxing – one of only a few contact sports you can do from a chair.

One day I was sick but I still took part in a boxing class. Everyone took a 'no excuses' attitude. Regularly I did about five hours of physical activity a day, only stopping for lunch in-between. Despite still being in my wheelchair I lost nearly a stone in ten days due to the sheer physical exertion. I examined my face and arms every day to see if I was losing weight as I could literally feel it dropping off me. It was hard work physically but it was worth it. My whole focus was to get fit and then get fitted with my prosthetic leg. As I'd committed to the London Marathon and told Milly I was doing it, there was no way I was letting her down and not taking part.

Even though there were times I felt I couldn't go on and every muscle in my body ached, I stuck with it. I felt I was starting to take control of my body again and this in turn was helping to focus my mind. My mood swings were starting to go and my outlook on everything was changing. Instead of being a novelty, sleeping well at night became the norm – I was so physically exhausted. My confidence grew massively and when I went home for a few days' rest I couldn't wait to tell Jamie and Milly what I'd achieved. It was a fantastic feeling and, mentally, I was transforming: the old me was coming back.

The medics at Headley Court try and get you on a prosthetic limb as quickly as possible. Your first leg is a leg in name only as it's more of a metal pole with a foot on the end. After just one week I had my first fitting at the prosthetics clinic. Barely able to sleep for excitement the night before, as I went down I thought: 'This is it, I'm going to get my leg and walk straight away!' In retrospect that was terribly naive. The brutal reality was that when the prosthetic was strapped around my stump and I was eased between the two parallel bars you are meant to walk between, I just fell to the ground – I was too fat to use my prosthetic. I just burst into tears and cried and cried. It seemed I was trapped in a vicious cycle – unable to exercise as I struggled to put weight on my new titanium leg – but without exercise unable to lose the weight.

Worse still was that after I'd had my leg amputated my body had gone into shock and all my hair had begun to fall out. It had started when I had a shower just a few weeks after coming out of the coma. Relaxing, letting the water wash over me, I began to shampoo my hair. When I started to lather it up a massive clump of my hair came out. I just screamed. It was lying there at the bottom of the cubicle. As the water rained down on me I stood there, crying.

'Oh, my God, can anyone throw anything else at me?' I thought. It was devastating. In fact, it was worse than losing my leg. It felt like my femininity was going. I was fat, I only had one leg and now I was going bald. The next three weeks were horrendous as each day I noticed more of my hair was falling out in clumps in the shower. It felt like every time I washed it more fell out.

Initially, I went to the doctor and said: 'My hair is falling out.' But as it's so thick it wasn't immediately apparent.

He said: 'It happens for lots of reasons like stress. Have you got any bald patches?'

I said: 'No,' as I didn't at that point.

'That rules out alopecia, then,' he replied. He seemed to think I was losing a few strands like women sometimes do at the end of pregnancy, not the sheer volume that was dropping out of my head. It came out in clumps from my hairbrush and out in the shower – huge amounts, balls of it. So I put a zip-lock freezer bag next to my bed to collect the tufts that kept dropping out. I wanted to show him the evidence of what was happening so he would understand this was anything but a few strands.

But I never needed to show him. By the time I went back to the doctor, it was clear all of my hair was going as I was left with only baby fluff on my head and a few long tufts. It looked like mange. I was pretty much inconsolable at that time and I feared it would never come back. He diagnosed me with telogen effluvium, a temporary form of hair loss brought on by surgery, major physical trauma or stress – so I ticked every box. I could barely bring myself to look in the mirror; it was devastating.

The nurses were brilliant; they told me from the start they were sure this was only a temporary thing and it was just my body's reaction to shock. I had a brilliant welfare officer at Headley Court, who had battled cancer, so she understood the impact it had on me straight away and she made enquiries about wigs. The charity Help for Heroes stepped in and paid for me to have human hair wigs until it grew back, which enabled me to face the world. I'd get up in the morning before putting on my wig and check my head. If I saw a few tufts of stubble I'd say, 'Oh, it's definitely grown a little bit – I've got a little bit more bum fluff!'

With the charity's help I was able to choose a blonde wig.

I got the wig fitted while I was on leave from Headley Court and when I came back all the guys were like, 'Wow, Hannah, you're blonde! I'm loving the new hair.'

I had to tell them not to be so daft – I was wearing a bloody wig! They wouldn't have known, though, until I told them but they were all brilliant about it and no one said anything negative. The medical staff were great as well and as I couldn't wear wigs to do physio, the nurses would try and plait the few chunks of hair I did have to make me look better. No one ever made me feel self-conscious. I think everyone felt really sorry for me after everything I'd been through as this was like a final kick in the teeth. Going bald was one of the few times in my life where I actually cried properly in front of people as I was just so gutted that it was happening to me.

I remember Nikki came round and I wailed: 'What else can be thrown at me? What the hell else do I have to go through?' She just hugged me and said that it was going to be all right and this was a small setback on my road to recovery.

Her kindness made me cry even more and I shouted: 'I'm the fattest, now the baldest one-legged woman out there! What on earth is coming next?'

The only thing that stopped me going completely off the rails about it all was the fact that my hair started growing back pretty much straight away, albeit in random tufts. Once I knew it wasn't going to last forever I even let Milly watch me put my wig on when she walked into my room. I didn't try to hide it. I just said: 'Mummy's hair is going to grow back and look, it's started already,' and I let her touch my stubble.

As soon as it got long enough I had hair extensions put in: first, blonde and then bright red. I found an amazing hairdresser near Headley Court, who would either come in or visit my house and sort everything out for me. After my hair grew back, I became much more conscious of it and I still am, in fact. I was so grateful to feel feminine again and it gave me a whole new understanding of what it means to lose that part of you, especially for a woman.

While dealing with my loss of hair I started to acknowledge the fact that despite still being nineteen stone, I needed to find a way to walk properly so I could fulfil my marathon dream. I had by that time managed to walk a few faltering steps between two metal parallel bars at the prosthetics department. It was agony on my new man-made limb but I felt despite my weight it was a start. The physio kept telling me not to do too much but once I get tunnel vision about something, there's no stopping me.

With massive exertion, after about four weeks of rehab at Headley Court I actually managed to walk down the corridor for the first time. Jamie had brought Milly in to pick me up, as it was the weekend. I slipped on the prosthetic and despite it being uncomfortable, I thought: 'I am damn well going to wear it!' Milly and Jamie stood waiting at the end of the corridor about 20 metres away, and for the first time I walked down to meet them.

I shouted: 'Hey, can't you notice anything? I've just walked down the corridor to meet you – I've started to walk again!'

Milly started screaming with excitement and Jamie hugged me and shouted: 'Oh, my God!' We were just so happy. It was an incredible moment. That was the first time Jamie had seen me walking properly in years. I don't think Milly had any memory of me walking before the blast – she was too young.

That weekend I went home with them and I just wouldn't take the leg off at all except when it was time to sleep. I was so desperate to learn to walk and so delighted to be upright for the first time in years. I was supposed to use crutches but I was so eager to get back to normal that I didn't bother with them. After I got my first prosthetic I rarely used my wheelchair again. Ironically, I'd been issued a custom-made wheelchair as I was finally disabled enough to need one. You are allowed to choose whatever you want so I chose luminous pink with a black trim. The company didn't do pink without you having to pay an extra cost, which Headley Court told me they wouldn't cover. The next best thing was black, although I felt a bit disappointed. Then, I got a phone call from the manufacturer, who said they'd decided not to charge me. So they made me this bright hot pink wheelchair, which now lives in my basement. While I do have to keep it in case I ever need to use it, I vowed never to get in it and to date I rarely have.

I had only been at Headley Court for a matter of months when I decided to spend some of my Army compensation money for my injuries on something just for *me*. After my initial payment in 2007 for my injuries, I received a second compensation payment in 2010 following the amputation of my leg and a diagnosis of phantom limb pain, which will trouble me for life and which can be a side effect of blast injuries. As part of my compensation I received an inflation-proof Army pension for which I'm incredibly grateful to the Army. The reality is that with my injuries I wouldn't be able to hold down a 'normal' job as I can't stand on my feet all day. Or if I got a skin infection in my stump, I'd have to take weeks off work, as I'd be off my leg. This payout meant I'd not face financial hardship in the future and while I'd still need to work, I could take a job that I'm physically able to do.

I rang Nikki and said to her: 'I've decided it's time for that holiday we talked about'. I spoke to Jamie and said: 'I'd love to have a girly holiday' and, as always, he completely supported me. I told him I want to treat myself and Jamie had said: 'If you can get yourself up and walking then you deserve it.' The hair extensions made me a bit less insecure so the time was right to take a Thelma and Louise style trip. I booked Paradise Island in the Bahamas, including a limo to pick us up from the airport with champagne – it was the most expensive holiday I've ever been on. It was unbelievable and I'd never experienced anything like it or seen people literally dripping with wealth like they were there – famous American Football stars, swimwear models dripping in Cartier diamonds – and us!

The team at Headley Court made me a special swimming leg and so, just a matter of months from when I'd learned to walk I was on a British Airways flight to the sun. My military ID card was in my passport and as soon as they saw it they upgraded us to First Class. The BA hostess at the end of the flight gave us a carrier bag full of mini vodkas and said: 'Girls, this is such an expensive holiday I've given you this – use the money you save to go and do an activity on us.' British Airways was so amazing they actually thanked us for our service over the tannoy on the flight and the passengers were clapping. They could not have been kinder to us. Nikki and I kept looking at each other saying: 'Wow, flying with BA is amazing!' Going with Nikki was brilliant. We spent days by the pool and I even managed to walk across sand – which is no mean feat as a newby amputee because it's so uneven. Nikki gave me the confidence to take off my leg as we sunbathed by the pool – and after initially being unable to relax, in case people were horrified, I quickly realized no one seemed particularly interested in me.

After a few days I was having a relaxing snooze, with my prosthetic propped up against my sun lounger, when I was awoken by the sound of a walkie talkie: 'Houston,' a little boy whispered urgently, 'we have a problem! Urgent assistance required.' I opened my eyes drowsily to see three cheeky little boys gasping at my prosthetic leg, in a mixture of fascination and horror. 'Hello!' I said. 'Do you want to see my robot leg?' and soon they were all fascinated and talking about it. Funnily enough, that gave me a bit of confidence, as I was so cripplingly insecure. But, of course, nothing ever goes to plan and later that night as we walked across the hotel reception, my amazing robot leg just snapped, sending me sprawling across the floor. 'Oh my God, Nikki, what am I going to do?' I said, thinking, I was thousands of miles from Headley and god only knows what I was going to do for the rest of the holiday with no leg.

'Wait there,' she said 'It's OK, it's fine.' And she literally pulled my spare leg out of her bag. 'I thought I'd better pack a spare just in case,' she laughed. Now that is a sign of a true friend – packing a spare leg secretly in her suitcase! The only downside was that my spare leg didn't quite fit as well, so air would get trapped and force its way out, making loud farting noises each time I took a step. So it was slightly awkward in that every time I walked around I made somewhat undignified noises. In the end I made light of it and I'd say: 'I'm sorry you must have heard me coming, excuse me, but my leg is farting.' And, thank goodness, the rest of the holiday was blessedly uneventful.

Shortly after returning from the Bahamas with Nikki, a wonderful opportunity came along. I was invited to take part in the Amputee Games, an event organised by Battleback, a charitable sports rehabilitation programme. So I signed up, just like everyone else. But before taking part I had a crisis of confidence: I thought everyone would be staring at the fat girl and I had to force myself to go. I did no formal training and just turned up at Stoke Mandeville sports ground, thinking I'd try out a variety of sports. Because I'd been lugging my twenty-one-and-a-half stone frame on crutches for the past three years, I had good upper-body strength but it still came as a surprise to everyone just how good I was at weight lifting. I started out pretty light and when I found it easy, the guy running the event said: 'I think you are pretty good!' So he entered me there and then for the competitive part of the Games.

Because I was still struggling to walk I'd wheel myself to the bar in my wheelchair and then stand up to get myself in position for the event. I sailed through stages one and two and then it came to the finals and, unbelievably, I won a gold medal! Somehow I managed a silver in archery and a bronze in rowing too – also down to my Russian shot-putter's physique! Afterwards, I was asked if I'd consider attending a talent-spotting event, where future Paralympians were often found, but I felt I'd reached my peak with that gold and I decided I didn't want to take it any further as I didn't think I'd be able to fit it around my life as a mum.

When I look back at photos of myself competing I'm speechless, really. There were a lot of factors that made me so fat, but ultimately I was responsible, as I put the cake in my mouth. But there are positives as well: I look at the old me and think that was the start of it all, the beginning of my journey back to recovery.

With so much going on I was surprised to be asked to attend a meeting in front of a board who wished to talk to me about Iraq. I sat at the opposite side of a boardroom table before a number of officers I'd never seen before. They asked me a series of questions about my experience of Iraq: whether I felt I had the right kit, how I'd been dealt with medically afterwards and what morale was like out there, and whether we were asked to do jobs that were appropriate to our skill level. At that time I was told it was to do with the Iraq Inquiry. I can only assume, prior to Chilcot, it was a fact-finding exercise and they wanted to speak to a broad spectrum of people to get a wide range of views about what was going on. I told them what had happened to me and that morale was on the floor when I was out there. How it was hard that Iraq is such an unpopular war with the public back at home and it's now gone to wrack and ruin. I felt I could have seen that coming while we were out there. Our boys were handing over to the Iraqi police force and quite a few of us felt that things were going to fall apart.

Back at Headley Court, things were great for me socially as well as the physical stuff. I met so many brilliant people, who are still friends now. I arrived at the same time as two other lads and the three of us immediately hit it off. We were all single amputees and all started off together in the wheelchairs. Our little gang would sneak off for cigarettes together and we were always getting told off by the instructors when we weren't where we were supposed to be. It was a laugh, like bunking off from class at school. There was a bar at the centre, just to give the place some kind of normality, and it was a great way to unwind and have a laugh and make friends. We'd be there every night, propping it up.

There was no stopping us as soon as we grew more competent on our legs. When we had finished our day we would head to nearby Epsom for a drink. Because I was with two other amputees I felt less self-conscious or embarrassed at being seen out with only one leg. People would sometimes stare at us but that was probably because we were a group of amputees. Together we just took it on the chin. At that point I didn't have a leg that looked like a leg – it was metal bar with a foot – but because I was with two friends who also had the same legs I knew I didn't have to worry as they would never have allowed anything to be said to me. I'd been so miserable before that to be able to go out again was a window into a world I thought I'd lost forever and I just went for it.

There was another great guy who used to come out regularly with us. He was a triple amputee and still used his chair, but he didn't let that hold him back in any way. One night he got so drunk he fell on the joystick that operates his chair and we found him spinning round and round outside the pub. I just though:, 'Oh, my God! If anyone sees this we are going to be in so much trouble!'

We used to cover for each other all the time if one of us was hungover. As there were three of us there was always one person who would make sure they'd told the instructor we were in prosthetics or somewhere else when really we were getting a couple of extra hours in bed. It sounds silly and trivial now but this whole after-hours' curriculum was all part of the rehabilitation process as we were entering back into normal life again. It was the first time in years many of us had begun to feel like normal people again, able to go to the pub to have a drink and a laugh just like everyone else. It was also a way to chat through how we were feeling emotionally and mentally and not just concern ourselves with our physical rehabilitation. Just sitting having a drink in a pub was not only a way to let off steam, it was a way people could feel they were letting their barriers down and to actually share stories with each other.

It was while we were on one of our nights out that one of the lads told me he had had a really odd out-of-body experience. We started talking about how out of it you are when you first come round and it's really common for a lot of guys to have no memories of the moment they were injured. Some do, but I always felt extremely lucky that I don't have to face the nightmare of those moments. He sort of dreamed, while he was still conscious and awake, that he'd been taken out of his body and put into another body, where he became a kind of super-soldier. He had to battle to get back into his body on earth. When he won the fight, that's when he came round. We started speculating about whether it's the painkillers you are given that lead you to vividly hallucinate, but I really don't think that was the case with me. Many of the severely injured have had experiences like that – it's really common – but only the ones who have been close to death. I'm not religious but I now think there is something else; however, I don't know what it is. I'd always described myself as an atheist, but I am more spiritual now than I was before. I don't think we cease to exist – I think a little drop of our essence as human beings carries on somewhere else.

If you had told me months before that I'd be able to open up with people I'd never met before and discuss things like that I would have laughed. I'd spent years becoming invisible in my chair and not engaging with life. But Headley Court was changing me physically and my mental outlook was certainly improving. I'd overcome the darkest of times and even though there were still moments when I was in that dark place, I could see light in my future. That's why I agreed to take part in a photo shoot with a rock star.

Three months after my amputation a journalist called Caroline Froggatt contacted me through the injured servicemen's charity Blesma and said: 'We are looking for a girl to take part in a photo shoot for a book, with pictures from it being put on display at the National Portrait Gallery. Would you like to come to Bryan Adams' house to take part?'

It was all a bit surreal but I said yes. Jamie drove us into London; we turned up at Bryan Adams' house, which I wasn't expecting. He had set up a studio in the vast basement of his house next to the River Thames. His wife had just had their first baby and she and Caroline opened the door and welcomed me in. There were a load of lads that I knew from Headley Court and some were already in the studio having their portraits taken. While in a group I'd discovered a newfound confidence that hadn't yet translated into life outside Headley Court, so when I walked in, I felt crippled with insecurity and really miserable. But I wanted to do it. To be honest, I don't know why, apart from the fact I was quite proud of my artificial leg as it meant so much to me because it had transformed my life.

Here I was, taking part in a professional photo shoot with Bryan Adams, yet I was totally miserable because of the way I looked. I had lost some weight by then, but it was a drop in the ocean compared to what I needed to lose and I was big. I sorted out my make-up as there was no stylist on the shoot as they wanted us to look natural and like we were in real life, and then Bryan came over and said hello. He was really friendly, explaining he wanted to capture me relaxed. There was a big team helping him, a vast array of cameras, flashes and photo-editing kit – the full shebang. I stood against a huge white infinity wall while he clicked away, talking all the time, only pausing to pose me in a new position, guiding me as to what he wanted me to do.

It was a real struggle, but I managed to stand on my prosthetic for long enough so he could take two sets of photos of me: one in a long black dress and a second set in military uniform. In both I showed my prosthetic leg. In front of the camera I was incredibly under-confident; at that point, with strangers, I struggled to even make eye contact as I was still battling with my self-esteem. But Bryan put me at ease as much as it was possible to do, which was no mean feat. He had no celebrity airs; he was just a lovely man. The bottom line is I just wasn't happy being the 'me' I was at that time. I didn't even ask to see any of the images on his camera.

Regardless of that, it was a lovely day. Bryan got everyone sushi for lunch and we ate with his family and then left. Jamie chatted the breeze over lunch, talking about football, where he'd been on his recent travels and asking about the cameras. I was pleased that I didn't have to do any of the talking – I felt painfully shy and introverted. When you've been in a wheelchair for three years you get used to people ignoring you and talking to the person who is pushing the wheelchair, so I'd become a person who didn't have to engage in life very much. Although I was walking on and off on my leg I still hadn't come out of the shell completely, so instead I just soaked up the atmosphere.

I didn't see Bryan Adams' photos until months later when

they were finally hung in the National Portrait Gallery and they asked me to attend. I received a lovely email saying, 'Would you like to come to the launch?' So I went online and had a look at the website and that's where I saw the photos for the first time. I was horrified. I just thought: 'Oh God, they're awful!' I was so upset. I absolutely hated them, so there was no way I was going to go and see them in the flesh.

A few weeks a copy of the book arrived from the publishers as a gift for me. I couldn't even stand to open it. It was as though every time I looked at the image I would be sucked back into hell. It was many months since I'd posed and I'd moved on by such an extraordinary degree: I was more confident but I still wasn't yet ready to confront how low and desperate I'd been at that time. I knew the image was undeniably powerful and it's a vividly accurate snapshot of where I was in my life in that moment. While I wasn't ashamed of that – it was such an accurate reflection of how I was feeling during that incredibly painful time – it was tough to see.

I only showed my mum and two of my closest friends the book but their most shocked reactions weren't about me, they were about the other soldiers in the book. They all said, 'Oh, my God, I didn't realise people survived such serious injuries!' Up until then I was the most injured person they'd ever met, but in comparison to other soldiers I've only got a scratch! So it's an incredible book for raising awareness. In the grand scheme of things I'm one of the least injured people I know out of all the guys I was with at Headley Court. It's a shocking, yet inspirational book.

Funnily enough, life got better from that day onwards for me. That said I'm unlikely to be in a place where I'd have the book on the coffee table at home. In fact, when my second daughter Lexi-River couldn't reach the floor in her baby bouncer, it's very ironic but the book, *The Legacy Of War*, was underneath her for the first six months of her life. I think it would be incredible if Bryan were to come back to us all five years on and really see how far we've come. Some of us were already on our journeys to recovery, but others, like me, were at the start of rehabilitation and rebuilding our lives. The only thing I wish is that I could tell the girl in the pictures what great things were just round the corner for her. A new life and a new beginning, and that the weight would go and I would be totally transformed beyond even my recognition.

CHAPTER ELEVEN

GASTRIC BYPASS

There is a side to my personality that if I set my mind to something then I will do it, no matter what. That dogged determination had made me one of the first groups of girls to join my local Scouts and later on decide to elope, then amputate my leg – and now it would help me make a drastic decision to ensure I'd run the London Marathon.

At the end of 2011, still obese, unhappy and struggling to walk on my prosthetic, I decided to tune in to watch *The Fat Doctor* on the Discovery Channel to see how people tackled their weight. On the show a British surgeon, Mr Shaw Sommers, performed a gastric bypass on a morbidly obese woman and she was unrecognisable within twelve months. I knew I needed to do something radical to get out of the rut I was still stuck in and I realised if I had surgery, I would be able to run. In my heart I knew a bypass would work for me as I had a certain relationship with food that had become ingrained over a lifetime. As a child I was always taught: 'Finish everything that's on the plate' and sweets were a treat. Once I'd become depressed food became a 'treat' to cheer myself up until it got out of control. It became my enemy then, and I was an addict, constantly craving my next fix of junk. I'd totally lost self-control.

That night I googled 'Gastric Bypass Surgery': I hated myself and was ashamed to be a size 24 and there was no doubt that my weight had contributed to my coma. More than anything I wanted to be able to walk to the shops, to the park with Milly and to complete my marathon milestone. Before returning to Headley Court for my next three-week period of rehabilitation I booked a private consultation with Mr Sommers. After a thorough examination, despite my medical history, he said he was prepared to help me. I was so elated. The cost was steep at £10,500, but I thought it was worth every penny to get my life back.

I was really anxious about speaking to the team at Headley Court as I was still serving and I needed permission to go ahead with the operation. I feared Army bureaucracy would stop me. To my surprise, they were very supportive and they gave me the green light as they recognised without it I'd struggle to ever walk anything other than very short distances. I had a break coming up in December 2011 for Christmas, so I booked myself in to have keyhole surgery. I used some more of my Army compensation money and it really was a no-brainer, the best cash I ever spent.

Mr Sommers bypassed part of my small intestine, which absorbs all the fats, sugars and nutrients you consume, then he stapled my stomach so that the only part that's useable is an area roughly the size of your thumb. You shed the fat in three ways. First, you have a tiny stomach, so physically you can't eat as much; you also have something called 'malabsorption', which means your body doesn't absorb the fats any more. Finally, if you try to cheat, you get something called 'Dumping syndrome', where because the part of the bowel that normally absorbs sugar is gone, the new bit of bowel absorbs sugars straight into your bloodstream and it overloads your system. This causes you to vomit, suffer dizziness and you foam at the mouth if you eat anything high in fat or high in sugar. Dumping syndrome is so unpleasant that it's like a cognitive therapy – it retrains your brain so it knows that if you put that chocolate bar in your mouth you're going to be sick. That means you don't eat as much, you don't absorb as much into your body and it helps with how you deal with food mentally.

I never experienced any problems because I was so motivated to lose weight, I didn't cheat and gorge myself on food, and post-surgery I had no complications. In fact, I healed really quickly and was up and walking the same day. The following day, I went home and the three incisions, one in my belly button and one each side of it, healed within a week. I was highly motivated and I didn't want to cheat, as I so desperately wanted to get thin. Instead of gorging on six bags of crisps a day, initially I had toddler-sized portions of mashed food before moving up to three small, normal healthy meals: Weetabix for breakfast, a sandwich of something like tuna salad for lunch and fish or meat with vegetables for dinner, and I'd still have the odd treat, like a packet of hula hoops.

The weight loss was so rapid that after six weeks I stopped weighing myself as there was no point in me getting on the scales. Within days, I knew I'd be lighter again. Jamie was so happy for me as he could see my mood lifting and my confidence slowly starting to come back. For him it was like he was getting the old me back and he couldn't have been happier. Now the pressure was off and all I wanted to do was get to a stage where I was happy with myself. Within three months I'd lost four stone, the junk food replaced by healthy homemade soups and salads from Marks & Spencer. I cut out bread and instead ate rice and quinoa and I got down to a size 16. At that milestone I decided then to bin all of my fattest clothes as I knew I would never, ever need them again. Pulling out the size 18s, 20s, 22s and 24s was cathartic and fantastic all rolled into one. It was my way of saying goodbye to the person I didn't want to be.

I kept one pair of size 24 trousers to remind me of how fat I was, which are still in my loft. Nikki and I found them recently and when we tried them on, she could stand in one trouser leg and I could stand in the other. I only suffered from Dumping syndrome once, which was caused by a cereal with a higher sugar content than I expected, and it made me violently sick. A year after surgery I also tried one square of chocolate and I felt ill again, so that took the temptation away. Dumping syndrome stops after three or four years as your body adjusts but it's done such a good job on me that it cracked my addiction to junk food. Where I used to eat three chocolate bars a day, now I'm happy with one chocolate bar a week. To me, putting two chocolate bars in my mouth isn't worth getting fat again. Feeling confident and good about myself is what motivates me now. Today I take multivitamins due to my malabsorption to ensure I get the nutrients I need and I still have a smaller stomach so I can't eat as much as other people, but that's a small price to pay.

Surgeons normally anticipate patients will lose a stone a

month, but my weight loss was kick-started as I was doing such intensive physio at Headley Court. It was like having the best-ever private trainer to get you into shape. This also meant I continued to get my independence back and, in turn, I started to feel better about myself. When I made it to a size 14 I went out and blew £250 on a pair of True Religion jeans. When I stood in front of the mirror I saw they fitted me perfectly. I'd never spent that much on jeans before but I wanted to treat myself to something other than food.

Within ten months I'd lost an astonishing amount of weight: eleven stone, and I'd got down to a size 12. Buoyed with newfound confidence I decided to sit my driving test at Headley. I'd never sat my test before as I hadn't got round to taking driving lessons, so this was a bit deal for me, but I was determined to have the freedom of being able to drive and go where I wanted, whenever I wanted. A lot of the lads splashed out on amazing cars when their compensation money came through – Porsches, BMWs – and many had personalised number plates. There was probably even a bit of competition over who had the best wheels. I thought: 'Fuck it, I want to be able to drive so I don't have to be dependent on anyone else to take me around!' As it's my left leg that has been removed, it actually wasn't that difficult for me to learn to drive as you do all the changing of brakes and stuff with your right. I blew an absolute fortune on a convertible Audi, spending more than £20,000 of my compensation money. With hindsight that was ridiculous. At the time it seemed worth every penny as I had so much fun with it and I really enjoyed the freedom of being able to razz around on my own. It was the first time in what seemed like forever I could be on my own and not need a carer with me. I was in charge of my own destiny again.

It may sound corny but I was literally getting back in the driving seat of my own life. Every day I would go out in the car and just drive around with the roof down, if the weather was good, and for the first time in absolutely years I felt free and like a weight was lifting from my shoulders. My hair was still coming back in patches at the time, so I wore a wig and I used to wear a bright headscarf to pin it down with. But one day I was tearing along the M25 with the roof down and my music blaring and my wig flew off, never to be seen again. I had to get off at a service station in order to find something to cover myself with. Flustered, I rung Jamie and told him my wig was now somewhere on the hard shoulder, or perhaps it had even hit someone's windscreen like a mysterious piece of roadkill! He just burst out laughing, as the scene in his mind's eye was so comedic. Thankfully, I always kept a spare wig in the car as I used to think you never know when you might need it, although I'd didn't expect it to disappear in quite such spectacular fashion.

Even being able to laugh at myself was such a big deal as it meant I was getting the old me back. If that had happened, even a few months before, it would have crushed me but now I was feeling so much more positive I could see the situation for what it was – a funny one! It was like I'd been reborn and nothing and no one would stop me from doing anything. I was free and I was going to enjoy every single second of life from there on in.

Too much of anything is bad for you, however, and at this time I went into a kind of overdrive and I went off the rails. Once I'd put Milly to bed I'd go out drinking and clubbing with the girls, desperate to make up for lost time, leaving Jamie to babysit. I was being selfish but it was only because

I'd put so much of my life on hold for so long that I was reliving the youth I'd lost. Burning the candle at both ends led to cracks appearing in my marriage as I wasn't devoting nearly enough time, or energy, to our relationship. I wanted to go out partying with old friends, get smashed and have a laugh – it was never about other men. I just wanted to let my hair down and be the old Hannah again. The flip side to this was that Jamie was spending more and more time at home on his own or working, as he was still serving with the REME, while I lived it up. Over a period of a few months it became obvious we were beginning to lead separate lives. Our sex life became virtually non-existent and instead of him being my carer, our relationship became more and more like a loving brother and sister. The passion had just gone out of it after everything we'd been through.

I think that period was really hard for Jamie for although I was still living in the same house and still his wife, I had all but left him. I felt I had so much catching up to do: I'd cheated death twice and it was my time to be reborn. It felt like up till then life had got it in for me and had pretty much turned into the film *Final Destination*, in which everyone is being haunted by death and they have to keep on running from it. Determined I was going to keep running, I planned to enjoy every second of what was left. I felt I could die any day so I was determined to go out with a bang.

Obsessed by that fact, I wanted Milly to have lots of experiences with me so she'd have happy memories. I splashed out on holidays to the Caribbean three times, a thermal spa in Slovakia, then a five-star trip to Turkey. It sounds insane but I just felt we had missed out on so much together as mum and daughter that I wanted to give her a bank of good experiences with me. As we lay on the latest beach I'd say to Jamie: 'If I die then I want Milly to have known me fit and well as I am now – not think of me as sick and unhappy in a wheelchair.' Jamie's response was: 'I'll always support your choices Hannah,' and he always did.

Despite jetting about to all these amazing destinations, all the while the cracks were getting wider in my marriage. It was a cruel twist of fate, really. Just as I felt like the past was slowly becoming the past and I was beginning to forge a healthy mother-and-daughter bond with Milly, my relationship with Jamie was being torn apart. Doing the simplest things like reading a book together or having an ice cream on the beach take on a whole level of new meaning when you think that maybe you shouldn't have been there or this might be the last time you do it. But in addition to that, there is nothing more liberating than living life exactly in the moment and that's what I was doing. I wanted Milly to be cultured and I wanted her to have been to the theatre. I wanted her to have experienced all of that stuff, so that's what I did – I packed in everything I possibly could.

After about six months I finally calmed down and started getting back to everyday life. I stopped going out all the time, but by then the damage between Jamie and me had been done. We didn't argue at all but we had grown so far apart by then that often we'd sit in different rooms, even to watch TV. Jamie had become my mate and nothing more. We still chatted, but as friends. There wasn't that spark between us anymore that makes something turn from a friendship into a relationship. In my heart I knew it was over and I think he did too.

So one night I sat him down and said I thought I'd better have this conversation with him. We had been sitting watching something nondescript on the TV and Milly was in bed and I said: 'I can't go on like this, I want more.'

Initially he said to me: 'I can give you more. Let's just try it as I don't want it to end.' There were no tears or raised voices or hysterics. We were both calm and despite what he said, I think he knew in his heart that it was over as well. I just left it that night and it sounds bizarre but we went back to watching TV. We actually muddled on after this for a few weeks as we were and didn't bring it up again, but it was the elephant in the room. Once I had actually verbalised it to Jamie, I knew there was no going back.

Jamie spoke to my mum during this time and told her what had happened and he was really upset about it. He admitted to her, 'I can't give her what she wants.' Mum never told me until years later. She and dad always loved Jamie; they are still in touch, and that was between them. I brought it up again and got him to admit that we had both begun to see each other as friends. I don't think either of us could get over everything that had happened if we were being truly honest with ourselves. While we loved and deeply respected each other, we weren't in love any more. Once that had been said we both knew there was no going back as there was nothing to go back to. It was ridiculously amicable, though, as we both still loved each other as friends; we'd been through so much that it puts your entire life in perspective, and, of course, we had Milly to think about.

We'd already booked a holiday with Milly and Jamie's daughter, who is Milly's half-sister, Laura, to the Turks and Caicos for Christmas 2011. Our marriage was over, but we decided we'd still go on holiday as a family with the kids. It was absolutely lovely; we carried on as normal but it was purely platonic. We'd go to the beach, go swimming and do everything as though we were a normal family. We had a family room and even shared a bed but that was our final holiday. We didn't tell the girls and they had no idea, so it was a happy holiday and a nice way to say goodbye to our marriage.

We faced it head-on in the New Year after we got back. Jamie continued to live in our home for a while as he was waiting for his new Army quarters to be ready at the start of February 2012. It wasn't a wrench for Milly as he was only two streets away and we could see his house from the back garden. He still came round to dinner, so we had a very civilised break-up. Often he'd come round to put Milly to bed – if not, he'd wave to her from his window at bedtime.

Right to the last he was a good husband. Things had just run their course and I will never know if what happened to me made a difference or if it would have ended anyway. We were very happy before my accident and I loved him so much when we got married, but it was one of those things. People grow apart and neither of us ever looked back. He is still an amazing father and without him and our relationship I would never have had our beautiful little daughter and I will always thank him for that.

Since our break-up we've bickered over little things, which is why we are exes. We always come out the other side and things go back to being fine, but we've had our moments – which are always minor disagreements over things like whether Milly should have the latest toy, as neither of us wants to spoil her.

Jamie went on to meet Vicki, who is an extremely good step-mum to Milly, taking her out on girly days, helping her with make-up and supporting her. We all try our best to co-parent Milly, which is what is important, and we get along.

As time has passed Jamie and I are no longer best friends, but we share a deep respect for one another and always will.

As well as starting anew as a single woman, rebuilding myself physically became a priority over this time. As an amputee you need to have a variety of legs in order to perform the everyday tasks that bipeds (people with two legs) take for granted, and knowing I was going to be single again, making sure I had all the tools to enable me to live independently became a priority. So in the bottom of my wardrobe, neatly stacked under the clothes rail, instead of shoes, I have legs. Five, to be exact – so I'm the six-legged lady!

At Headley the first leg I was given was my 'everyday' leg, which is titanium with a shock-absorbing foot. While it's not the prettiest leg in the world, it's functional and great for running about every day, shopping and doing the school run. It's my 'workhorse' leg and the one I wear most often. My 'everyday' leg is the one that got me back on my feet again, but once I was walking I longed to be able to wear high-heeled shoes. Even though I was still in the early stages of my prosthetics I was given a prosthetic with an adjustable heel, which meant with the click of a switch I could move the position of the foot into an angle to fit the shoe I wanted to wear. For the first time in years I was able to slip on a pair of high heels. It sounds such a simple thing but to me it was life transforming. All I'd dreamed of since getting injured was getting back into my heels and this leg meant I would be able to make it a reality.

While spiky Louboutins were still a no-no, I remember the first pair of heeled shoes I bought. I'd only had the leg a few days and I was desperate to get to Russell & Bromley. I remember walking into the shop with Nikki and thinking,

'Oh, my God, I can buy something from here and actually wear it!' I picked up lots of high heels but finally settled on a pair of sexy black wedges as I needed some heel to give me support, since I have no sensation from the amputation onwards. I didn't even try them on because I was scared that they wouldn't fit or I'd fall over and make a fool of myself in front of the shoppers and staff.

As soon as I had paid we went straight back to the car and raced back to mine so I could try them on. Nikki started laughing as I literally ripped them out of the box in my lounge, clicked the switch on my prosthetic and slipped them on. I was close to tears when I looked down and saw my feet in a beautiful pair of heels. Even though a relatively small wedge, to me they seemed like the highest of stilettos. For the first few minutes I was a bit like Bambi, but once I'd got into the swing of it I could walk without any struggle at all. I had a full-length mirror in my hallway and I walked over to it and just stared at my feet, laughing for a couple of minutes. Finally I was in heels and I couldn't believe it.

Now of course it seems almost funny the way in which I bought this first pair of heeled shoes so quickly and surreptitiously as I didn't want anyone to know I was an amputee. Now I'm so confident I would think nothing of striding into any shoe shop with one of my false legs in my bag, whipping it out and trying the shoes on it. And while I'm no Imelda Marcos, I've got some great shoes, including Russell & Bromley over-the-knee boots, a pair of Vivienne Westwood heels... more pairs than I care to mention.

But when the world of high-heeled shoes opened up to me, it also meant I had to practise other things. One of the biggest were escalators in shopping centres. This was a massive deal as I was terrified I'd put my false foot down and the escalator would take it off and leave me doing the splits. It sounds really silly but I was so worried that my occupational therapist took me out in Epsom and we rode up and down the escalators. When I stood at the top for the first time I was shaking with fear but after I'd done it once I was fine. The funny thing is no one really bats an eyelid about it either. I think because I've accepted who I am and give off a positive vibe about it then so too does everyone else.

While my 'everyday leg' getting me walking again was a massive moment, equally as big was when I got a leg that looked like a real leg. Some of the guys at Headley Court were completely comfortable wearing shorts with their titanium legs on show, but I never was. Before the blast I'd always been a girly girl and I wanted to have a leg that made me look and feel as normal as possible, so the prosthetics team had one made for me. As soon as it arrived and some of the other guys saw how lifelike it was, they straight away wanted one of their own. It was what we all jokingly called 'Leg Envy' – when one person gets one type of leg then everyone else wants one too! I've seen blokes argue over special ski legs and when one said to the other, 'Why haven't I got that type of ski leg?' the answer was, 'Because you don't ski, mate!' It's light-hearted banter but it also helps keep you motivated and interested in what you're doing, how your body is, and how your legs can improve function and what you can achieve.

My first skin-coloured leg wasn't even that realistic looking but it caused quite a stir. Everyone wanted to have a look at it, see what it was made of and how natural it looked. But then one of the lads was getting married and as he was Scottish, he wanted to wear a kilt and so the prosthetics team specially made him an HD or 'high definition' leg. It was incredible and just like the real thing, even down to the veins, skin texture and tiny hairs. When I saw the pictures of his wedding – as the kilt covered the top of his stump you never would have known – I had 'leg envy' of my own. 'I am getting one of those HD legs made,' I thought. This was only a few months in at Headley and the prosthetics team kept saying you have to wait as you first have to stabilise with the leg you've got, not rush onto another leg, but I couldn't wait and so I forced them into ordering one for me, costing £15,000. When it arrived, it was just incredible. I stared at it for ages and I was almost afraid to touch as it was just so lifelike, even down to having tiny little veins, freckles and a few moles. It was, and still is, my favourite leg – if you can't see the join where it is attached to my stump then there is no way you would ever guess it's not my real leg.

I also got a 'water leg', which I can use for showering and swimming. As you'd guess, it's just like my everyday leg, except it's waterproof. That enabled me to start using showers again, regaining another part of my independence. Funnily enough, my HD leg allowed me to do Captain Kate Philp a small good turn after all she'd done for me. After I posted up some photos of myself wearing it, she contacted me via Facebook as she was interested in getting one herself and wanted to know my views. I told her how life changing it had been and how I'd really recommend it, as it had given an extra boost to my confidence. Later, I saw a photograph of her and she had one as well, so I like to think I've been able to help her a little bit after she was so good to me. We were both in such a unique position as females in the Army and it's so important to support to each other.

As I grew in confidence I started taking care of myself again. I had make-up tattooed on and then some fillers, which has so far cost me £3,000. I also started having Botox because my eye had dropped slightly, due to my facial injuries, and it puts it back into position. I also felt that all I went through had aged me prematurely. While I recovered from telogen effluvium and my hair grew, I also tried a dazzling array of new hairstyles that set me back £5,000 in total, although I've now got a full head of my own hair again. I also decided to go under the knife again, using some more of my compensation money and so I booked to have a boob job in February 2012 – just twelve weeks before I ran the London Marathon. I didn't tell anyone beforehand as I knew my mum would worry about me undergoing any type of procedure after all my body had been through. I just needed to do it for me. I'd lost so much weight that my breasts had lost volume. They weren't saggy, it was much worse than that: they resembled two deflated, wrinkly balloons. I'd scoop up the empty tissue into minimiser bras to disguise it, but without them I was quite badly disfigured.

The surgeon recommended I have a natural look so I went from a deflated C-cup to a D-cup to put back the volume I'd lost, costing £6,500. With hindsight it wasn't the wisest move so close to the marathon, but I was sure, as I normally recovered so quickly from my ops, that I would be fine for the big day. The operation was a great success and when I unwrapped the bandages, I loved my new boobs as they just looked 'normal'. 'That's another box ticked for getting back me,' I thought. They looked so natural that if you hadn't known about my weight loss, you wouldn't have realised I'd had a boob job at all.

I had two weeks of rest after the operation but then I made a foolhardy decision: I agreed to go ski-bobbing (like a bike that has two skis instead of wheels) with Blesma and fourteen other injured lads in Austria. I didn't tell them I'd just had implants because I knew they wouldn't let me go as your implants can slip until they settle in. I didn't want to miss out on any opportunity as every goal I accomplished was another brick in rebuilding my shattered inner confidence.

For the first few days I had an amazing time but I kept falling off spectacularly as they hit ridiculous speeds of up to 60 miles an hour. Then as I came off during one run and ended up rolling around in the snow, I actually felt one of my implants slip. I thought: 'Ouch!' but put it to the back of my mind until I returned to my hotel room. Later, when I got back, I looked in the mirror and to my horror I realised that something was very wrong as my breast looked wonky, flat and out of shape. I was a bit freaked out but I thought: 'That wasn't like that before.' I had a good feel of it and realised one of the implants had flipped over inside me. After a wave of initial panic I thought: 'What can I do?' I decided I'd have to move them round myself so I took some paracetamol and gritted my teeth. I'd been through worse in my life and I just knew I had to get on with it. After a few seconds of tugging and pushing I managed to manipulate the implant around underneath my skin and flip it back over into its correct position. You aren't supposed to be able to flip them like pancakes, but I'd clearly messed the operation up by doing something so strenuous. I was shaking and the sweat was forming on my forehead but I felt a wave of euphoria as I realised I was able to move it back into position. I then had to do the other breast, which also, thankfully, went back into place.

Afterwards I just thought: 'You absolute idiot!' I couldn't believe I'd been so stupid but that didn't stop me from continuing to ski-bob the following day. During the trip, the David Guetta song 'Titanium' came out and whenever it was played everyone would get their prosthetics out, so it became our anthem. In the end I won a silver award for passing the skills needed for the sport and even a special award for the 'Best Style' – which was for my technique rather than my outfit. But my competitive spirit had cost me dearly at the same time for it had completely botched up my new breasts and I knew this would be the start of yet more surgery to correct my foolhardiness. Still, I was determined to carry on with my sporting prowess and the next stop was the London Marathon that I'd promised to do all those months before from my hospital bed.

The day was dawning and I was ready for it.

CHAPTER TWELVE

MARATHON

My breasts were in agony from the moment I came back from the ski trip. I knew I should probably have gone to see a doctor, but I was scared that they would tell me not to do the marathon, which was only weeks away. The pain became so much and my chest was so sore, I decided to wing it without doing any running training. I convinced myself it would be fine as I was reaching the peak of my rehab at Headley Court.

While a big part of doing the marathon was the physical challenge, something – or more accurately someone – else, also massively motivated me as well. For years I'd felt I failed Milly as a mother and I desperately wanted her to be proud of me. Doing the marathon was to achieve something for her, as well as myself. So while not being able to do the practice I wanted was a blow, I was determined to make it over the finish line no matter what, even if that meant crawling on my hands and knees.

There was another reason why I wasn't able to run anyway. The final, vital, piece of equipment I needed in order to take part in the race was still being fabricated: a spanking-new custom leg with electric blue tiger stripes on it. Headley Court had agreed to make me my first-ever titanium running blade, just like you see Paralympians such as Richard Whitehead wearing. When it arrived, I was almost squealing with excitement. It was a bit like opening a longed-for Christmas gift as a child. I'd chosen it months before when I'd suffered from a massive bout of 'leg envy' at Headley Court on seeing someone who was further down the line in their rehabilitation wearing one in the prosthetics department. As soon as I saw him running around the track I'd said: 'I'd really like one of those legs.' So I had fittings for one, trialled a test version, and since then I'd chosen the pattern I wanted on the socket from a selection of swatches, like choosing curtain fabric. I had to go down to the prosthetics department at Headley to get it, and my occupational therapist was yapping away and all I wanted to say was: 'Yeah, can you just please go and get my leg!' Then she disappeared out in the back room for ages, as there must have been loads of prosthetic legs to sift through, before carrying it into the room.

As soon as I saw it 'in the flesh', so to speak, I thought: 'Ooh, that looks brilliant!' and I couldn't wait to get on it. It was weird putting the leg on as it's incredibly light, but it fitted me like a glove. As soon as I was helped to my feet I was way too cocky and thought to myself: 'Well, this can't be too hard, I've seen people running on these.'

My occupational therapist warned me: 'Don't just go running off, Hannah, as you need to learn to control it. We have to learn to walk on it first.' But it was too late.

'Pah, I can do this, how hard can it be? I've run before,' I thought. Immediately I tried to sprint off, boinged sideways and ended up flat on my backside in an undignified heap, thinking, 'Thank God I fell on my bottom and not my boobs – I should probably have listened.' After dusting off my pride I got straight back up and tried again as attempting 26.2 miles without the blade simply wasn't an option.

Basically, you have to treat the blade as a coiled spring, which is going to propel you forward more than a leg will. It's so springy that if you don't know what you are doing, it can actually ping you off in any direction like a Pogo stick. So it's all about controlling the power and that's what I didn't do with my first bounce. I learned which muscles to engage, the way in which you need to hold yourself and even how you use your other foot, as the blade is set in such a way it's like being on tiptoes so you have to run on the ball of the other foot to balance yourself. It was like learning to run from scratch all over again, using a completely different technique to the one I'd used all my life.

Within that first hour-long session I started to grasp the basics and technique and I was literally up and running. On day two I had a massive fall in front of all the lads when I tried to race someone. We were trying sprints up and down the gym and I was quite good and quite impressed with myself, so I got overconfident and I had quite a spectacular fall, completely face down. I did that really embarrassed motion of picking myself up at lightning speed and walking off – I didn't want the lads to see it had hurt so much, it brought tears to my eyes. I was also a bit panicked that my implant might pop out of position again, but I checked in the ladies loos and thank God, it hadn't. Falling hurts, so you learn really quickly not to, for an even greater fear was if I fell and damaged my stump, I could write myself off my leg and then I wouldn't be walking, let alone running, for weeks. My marathon dream would lie in tatters.

From that point on I used the blades for one hour every day for the next six weeks. Using muscles in a whole different way is so exhausting it quickly became clear I wouldn't be able to build up the stamina to do the whole route on my blade. I decided to divide the marathon into sections, running some of it on the blade and then alternating by power walking on my high-intensity prosthetic, which has an inbuilt shock absorber. I also realised I needed someone who was fit and able, someone I would listen to and not fly off the handle with, to support me. So when a high-ranking officer at my barracks offered to run with me, I agreed. As well as motivating me, he'd carry whichever leg I wasn't wearing at the time sticking out of the top of his backpack. We also decided he'd push my wheelchair for the whole route, just in case things really unravelled and I couldn't run or walk any more.

The truth is the sight of that wheelchair was enough to keep me on my feet. I never wanted to be that fat, invisible woman who sat inside it again. I just thought: 'After everything I've been through I might be winging it but there's no way I won't do it.' We did some long walks together in the lead-up to the race to find my pace and apart from that the only real preparation I made was researching how I could up my calorie intake before and during the run. Because of my gastric bypass I was unable to eat huge bowls of carbs or take on high amounts of sugar or I would suffer from Dumping syndrome and fall ill midway through. So we did loads of research and found a really high-calorie gel made up of whey and protein that gave me the calories I'd need without the sugar.

We stayed in a hotel the night before and I barely slept a wink, as I thought no one really expected me to complete it. On the morning I couldn't eat, as I was so nervous – I had such butterflies, I think I went to the loo ten times! One of the biggest 'prep' things I did before the race was to put on some Spanx control pants. I had to wear them because the loose skin around my tummy, due to my massive weight loss, wobbled and rubbed so much it would have chafed. I also put on two sports bras to hide my wonky boobs, as big boobs are a curse to exercisers! And I managed to hide it well under a Blesma T-shirt so nobody would have known.

I saw Milly briefly with my family while I collected my pass to get into the 'holding area' at Greenwich Park. My nerves were soon replaced by a steely determination as one of my family members, I can't remember who, said: 'If you have to drop out, don't feel like it's the end of the world. We'll still be proud of you, even if you get 10 miles round.'

I smiled politely but inside I thought: 'How dare you!' They did me a favour as that turned the nerves in my belly into a fiery determination – I wanted to make them eat their words.

I gave Milly a kiss and said: 'I'll be looking out for you all the way round. Make sure you are waiting for me at the finish line so we can go and get my medal.' She was so excited and when she said: 'I'll see you there, Mummy,' that fired me up even more.

I was waiting, nervous as hell, at Greenwich Park, where everybody congregated in preparation, waiting to be called to the start line, when a really enthusiastic Blesma lady said: 'Oh, I forgot to mention, we've got you an interview on the BBC.'

I said: 'Oh God!' as I hadn't put on any make-up, my hair was scraped back in a harsh plait and I didn't feel ready to go on TV at all. The next thing I knew, I was thrust in front of the camera for the first time in my life. I can't even remember what I said. Then it was straight on to the start line and I waved goodbye to Milly, thinking, 'Just watch me do this,' and the race began.

It took ages to cross the start line as there was just a sea of people in front. It took the first few miles for me to get into a rhythm and then I had two strategies: the first of which was to harness my competitive spirit and pick people off from the back all the way through. So I'd spot someone in the crowd as my target and then push myself forward. A few miles in I remember seeing a familiar figure in the crowd: James 'Arg' Argent from *The Only Way Is Essex*, who looked like he was struggling a bit. I love *TOWIE*, but I still had a chuckle to myself as I cruised past him.

As the miles clocked up, I ran past a lot of women who were really overweight and I was motivated to pass them as it was like leaving behind the person I used to be. That's not to say I thought ill of them; in fact as I went past them I thought to myself: 'Good on you! I've been there and everyone has got to start somewhere.' I recognised in them a lot of myself as I was once that fat person plodding along, and look how far I'd come.

I remember shouting encouragement: 'Come on, keep going!' to one woman who I really identified with as she was pushing herself hard and she was feeling the pain. When you are big you are quite self-conscious of running as everything jiggles, so I felt proud of them, even though I didn't know them, as they were doing something about it while doing something for charity as well.

My other tactic was to do as much as I could on my running blade, particularly on the faster parts of the course, such as the long flat Mall. But I had to change legs regularly as I wasn't proficient enough to use it for hours on end. For each leg change I'd sit on the kerb, whip my leg off and then put the other one on. I have to admire Paralympians as it's a real skill to use it in such a way that you can do the whole 26 miles on one leg.

The first five miles of the race went by in a blur. All my family were watching and they travelled around London to shout to me at different points. Milly was shouting: 'Mummy! Mummy!' and I took delight in passing by, running with my empty wheelchair alongside me, giving them a wave. But as well as Milly, a total stranger, Clare Lomas, also inspired me to keep going. She was called The Bionic Woman as she competed that year in a bionic suit to help her walk as she was paralysed. I thought she was incredible. The crowds were also amazing. Strangers who had seen me earlier on the BBC started shouting to me: 'Go on, Hannah, you can do it!' Blesma were also at different points so there was always someone to cheer you on every mile you clocked up.

Then, at the 10-mile mark disaster struck as my stump started swelling, which made it difficult to swap over legs. In the seconds it took to get it out of one socket and into the other it swelled so much, I couldn't get it on. I panicked a bit, so I sat in my wheelchair and forced my leg into the socket of my high-impact leg. From that point I couldn't change legs any more, so it became physically harder as I no longer had the 'spring' of my blade.

At 19 miles, I hit the wall. I thought to myself: 'Oh, my God! I've got another 7.2 miles to go!' But the Headley Court 'no excuses' mentality pushed me on. I told myself that scores of people have gone through Headley's doors and I needed to do them proud, plus I'd felt worse pain following the blast and my leg amputation. 'Keep going, keep going' I told myself to the rhythm of my foot and 'Milly's watching, you can't let her down' until I got a second wind. It becomes a mental battle at that stage and not a physical one. Anybody is capable of doing a marathon, even if it's walking it, but you've got to have it in your head: 'I am not going to stop.'

The final two miles from the 26-mile mark were the worst of all as I was so near, yet so far. I kept telling myself: 'You are not going to give in and let everybody think you only said you were going to do the marathon because you were drugged up to the eyeballs in hospital.' There was no way I was going to drop out so Milly would have to tell people: 'My mummy did three-quarters of a marathon.' The marathon was about me saying: 'Do you know what, I might have one leg, but fuck you, two-legged people, because I can do more than you!' I wanted Milly to be able to go to school and tell her friends: 'My mum did a marathon with one leg,' and to see that not having a leg was not detrimental in any way to living a normal life. I wanted her to think: 'My mum's got one leg but so what? I bet your mum hasn't run a marathon and she's got two.' Most of all I wanted her to be proud of me. That's what drove me round the final excruciating stage, although that final point-two of a mile seemed longer to me than the entire race.

When I got to the finish line and I couldn't actually walk another step, I was on my knees. Blood poured out of the top of my prosthetic liner on my leg every time I put my foot down because I'd blistered my stump so badly pushing myself to my absolute limit. It was so bad it was squelching and making really bad farting noises every time I took a step, which was attractive. Mum and Dad were waiting at the finish with Milly, who was holding the foil blanket. I let out a huge gasp of relief as I crossed the line and she wrapped it around me before saying, 'Mummy, you've just done a marathon!' She was so excited.

Mum and Dad told me how proud they were of me and then I collected my medal with Milly, who kept asking: 'Let me see your medal, Mummy!'

So I gave it to her and I said: 'I did this for you', so she got to wear it and show it off to everyone.

There was a reception at a local hotel at the end of the race for all the people who had run for Blesma. As it was impossible for me to walk any further, they got me a rickshaw, which, as you can imagine, was quite a feat with all the crowds at the finish line of the London Marathon. Once we got to the venue there was a sports therapist who was performing massage on all of the people who took part. I couldn't even take my leg off because if I did, it would have swollen so badly I wouldn't have been able to get it back on, so I hobbled around for a while and kept it on until I got home.

At the do, Milly said to me: 'Everybody's told me you are really brave, Mummy, and that you've done really well,' as if she really thought: 'Well, that's what they say.' So she had me in fits of laughter.

The minute I got home I took my leg off and got into the bath. My stump was completely raw and I had huge, angry blisters. Completely exhausted but elated at the same time, as I lay in the hot water, I thought: 'That's another box ticked so now I can get on with the rest of my life.' I couldn't walk on my prosthetic for two weeks afterwards, but it was worth it. And my boobs had held up – but only because they were already so far gone it really couldn't have got much worse.

Three days after completing the run I relegated my wheelchairs to the basement of my house. I had two hot-pink wheelchairs as the one they initially made me at Headley Court was made to fit my twenty-one-and-a-half-stone frame. When I lost all the weight it was no longer the right size for me so I had to get another, smaller wheelchair. After the marathon, I said: 'It's time for the wheelchairs to go.' It was another huge moment because I didn't ever want to use either of them again. Both are still in my basement with all the junk that I don't use any more.

The only time I spoke about taking part in the marathon again was two weeks later when I went back to Headley Court for rehab and I told the lads: 'I did the London Marathon the other week.' They said: 'Did you really?' I was so glad I did it, but ultimately, it was just the start of a whole new world opening up for me.

A month later I went back to work, doing the admin job I'd done before I was injured, in Bulford, which I combined with continued three-week stints of rehabilitation at Headley Court. I was incredibly uptight and nervous about returning to work as I'd been out for so long and I worried about how I'd be viewed as an amputee. But my new colleagues were incredibly supportive and it was good for me as I needed to go and face my demons about what going back to work in the Army meant.

At first I took a 'suck it and see' approach to decide if Army life was still for me. I hadn't known anything else since I was seventeen years old. On the one hand I desperately wanted to go back, but it was still incredibly daunting after all that had happened. It was great to be around people, I loved the social side and it continued to help me grow in confidence. I was no longer the bystander in my own life, watching the world pass me by from a wheelchair, and it felt good. The admin role meant I worked pretty much nine to five, so I was a normal working mum, spending all my free time with Milly and cherishing every minute of it, as I knew that's what mattered.

Six months after the marathon someone from Blesma rang me and said: 'Do you fancy skiing with us in Colorado?' Even though I'd never skied on two legs, let alone one, I said: 'Yes, please!' and my Commanding Officer was happy to support me going. Headley Court supported me so much in every way, as rehab was as much about building confidence on my legs, as well as self-confidence. Meeting up with all the boys again, many of whom I knew from Headley Court, was great. British Airways upgraded us all to First Class, gave us champagne and really looked after us all, which was out of this world.

After checking into the hotel we all met up for a few glasses of wine in the bar, where I made quite a splash. A few glasses of chardonnay, combined with the champagne on board and jet lag, left me drunk as a lord and I knocked over a Christmas tree in the hotel reception. Because of that shameful incident I was nicknamed 'Geoffrey'. I haven't got a clue where the name came from but it stuck and everyone found it hilarious at the time.

On the first morning, and nursing a hangover, we were given all the kit we needed to ski. My first question was: 'How do you get a ski boot on a prosthetic foot?' and the answer was simple: put a carrier bag on it first so you can slip it in and out.

I was totally relaxed until I got to the nursery slope, and

even though it wasn't that steep, inwardly I was freaking out. I felt more confident about doing the marathon than I did about being able to ski, so I said to Brendan West, the guy who organises the trips for Blesma: 'I'm really shitting myself. What if I can't ski?'

He laughed and said: 'Come on, Geoffrey, you'll be fine – you can do it.'

With that a triple amputee snowboarded straight past me and I thought: 'OK, if he can do it, I've got no excuses.'

Then someone else whizzed past, doing one-track skiing – where you ski using just one leg without your prosthetic – shouting: 'Come on, Hannah, it's amazing!'

So I decided then I couldn't bottle out and in truth, I didn't want to. The first hurdle I had to overcome was using the button lift, which is a challenge in itself with a false leg. I had to slide the rubber disc between my legs all the while trying to manoeuvre my ski on a foot I couldn't feel. A few times I rolled off, but because every one of us had two instructors that was a real security blanket as I knew I wasn't going to go whizzing off, down a mountain, unable to stop myself. They had me skiing on baby slopes within an hour of conquering the ski lift. Admittedly I wasn't following all the rules while I was going downhill and staying upright, but I did it. I fell over more times than I can recount but I loved every minute and it was another moment of 'It doesn't matter that I only have one leg, I can do this', which was just incredible.

I saw Brendan at lunchtime and he said: 'How was it?'

'It is absolutely brilliant! I'm loving it!' I replied.

The trip was for ten days, and I skied all day and got drunk every night and it was good for everyone. One guy, who was a double amputee, had been a bit in his shell at the start of the week, but by the end he was the life and soul, whizzing down the slopes at breakneck speed in a skiing chair.

Towards the end of the week there was a fancy-dress party, so my roommate and I decided to get the bus to Walmart to buy stuff for our costumes. We were both like Bambi on ice as you can't feel a thing with a prosthetic in snow boots and I was dressed, of course, as a Christmas tree with about 25 feet of garlands draped around me. My roommate was dressed as an elf so she was dubbed: 'Geoffrey the Christmas Tree's Little Helper' by the lads. Just getting out and doing stuff on our own was a confidence booster.

Flying home I thought: 'I've done a marathon and I can ski now and I couldn't even do that with two legs.' It all reaffirmed in my mind that I could have a normal life.

But there was just one thing I still wanted to do – and it involved going back to have surgery. I'd been so energetic that I'd continued to lose weight but my waist size was much bigger than it should have been as I had a lot of excess skin on my stomach from where previously I'd been much fatter. Now it wasn't plumped up by all the surplus weight I'd been carrying around, the skin had become crinkly and creased and there was an apron of tissue that no amount of exercise would shift. It was uncomfortable, it had rubbed me raw during the marathon and the ski trip and it was debilitating to lug this excess skin around with me.

So, I decided to have a tummy tuck costing £10,500, using more of my Army compensation money. It would be painful – but not compared to what I'd already been through. It was really important to me to have it done, as while I'd reconstructed myself mentally, I wanted to reconstruct myself physically too. I told my mum before the op and she was really concerned about me electing to have another round of surgery.

She said: 'Hannah, I've got your best interests at heart and I'm worried at how much your body can take.'

And I said to her: 'Mum, can you imagine what it's like to have to stuff skin into your trousers every day when you are in your twenties? I just don't want to do that for the rest of my life.' She also knows me and I was going to do what I was going to do.

So while she expressed her concern at me having yet another operation, when she heard my views she said: 'While I think it's a lot for your body to take, ultimately it's your decision.'

Again I found a very reputable surgeon and as he examined me I said: 'I don't mind a vertical scar, so can I have a fleur-de-lis?' This procedure involves two incisions, across your bikini line and vertically from under your boobs down the tummy, and the skin is pulled tight around your torso, as well as vertically. It's especially for people who have a lot of excess skin but it's not for the faint-hearted. I wasn't worried about the scars as my tummy was already covered in silvery lines from all the surgery I'd had previously.

Right away he said: 'Absolutely, that is the right procedure for you, it will really make such a difference.'

He booked me in only a couple of weeks later. I wasn't nervous at all – I just wanted to look normal again. He came to see me once I came round after the op and said: 'Look down and feel the skin.' It was so taut, he was obviously pleased with the job he'd done and I was thrilled to see I had a perfectly flat tummy. It even appeared neater than before as he'd been able to cut away a lot of the scarring I'd had from my life-saving surgeries and shrapnel injuries. There were roughly seventy dissolvable stitches. I was in quite a bit of pain afterwards and you have to wear a surgical corset for six weeks, so Jamie helped me and had Milly at his house so I could recover at home.

Ultimately, it was the cosmetic operation that changed my life the most as I no longer had this unsightly sagging skin to tuck in every day. For me that was a massive moment; it gave me huge amounts of body confidence and it felt like I was slowly becoming me again.

After I'd recovered from the surgery, I went motor biking with the charity Bike Tours for the Wounded along Route 66 in America. It was great to be one of the lads again. We all rode pillion on Harley-Davidson motorbikes and my rider had speakers so he blared out rock music as we sped through the Nevada desert. Before the tummy tuck I'd have been sore from my excess skin but this was something I was able to enjoy as a 'normal' person (albeit an amputee). And riding along I felt my body was no longer a prison – I felt truly free. 'This is one of those life moments which are absolutely amazing,' I thought to myself. While standing at the side of the Grand Canyon I burst into tears, it was so beautiful. I'd never seen anything like it before and I felt so small and insignificant. I thought: 'God, in the grand scheme of life, things really aren't that bad.'

At Headley Court I also learned to play sledge hockey, the only full-contact ice sport using a sledge that has one ski under it. You have a shortened hockey stick, you wear a helmet with a cage and full-body armour and you're allowed to hit your opponent anywhere you want to. All the boys took great delight in hitting me everywhere they could, pushing me over, so I spent half the time on my side on the ice, as getting upright is a total nightmare.

I also went indoor ski-diving for the first time, which was really good, and they had a surf machine, where I rode the air. I wasn't very good, but I did everything I could so I could go home and tell Milly the stories, and each achievement was also another building block of confidence. Shortly after I returned from the US trip in 2013, I completed my rehabilitation at Headley Court. They must have done a good job in giving me my confidence back as instead of wanting to blindly cling on, I knew I didn't love the Army anymore. For me it didn't have the same draw it once had, mainly because physically I struggled to achieve what I had before I was injured.

Then, when I was told that my unit was going to deploy to Afghanistan the following year, it became a watershed moment for me. I was able to do a lot of PT, which was great, and some new fitness tests had been brought in especially for amputees so I knew if I could pass it, they would consider me for redeployment. But there was an insurmountable hurdle: the moment I was told about Afghanistan, I knew I didn't want to go for I would never leave Milly again. Deep down, I knew with my amputation that I would struggle to function as a soldier on deployment – from the basics of trying to keep my stump clean to prevent infection to the fact that I would find it harder to defend myself with my prosthetic limb.

I didn't want to spend the rest of my career sat behind a desk – that wasn't what I joined the Army for. Thanks to the Headley Court rehabilitation and charity support I had achieved more than I'd ever thought possible. Yet I also recognised that physically I couldn't give the commitment to the Military that it needed. I couldn't be completely dedicated to the job as my heart wasn't in it because I wasn't able to do the job as well as I once had because of my injuries. Because of that it didn't hold the same draw and it wasn't for me anymore. That, combined with the fact my priorities had changed and I knew I wanted to be there for my daughter, meant I recognised my career was coming to an end. Going back to work was another thing I had to tick off my list on the road to being ready to get out of the Military, as it meant I knew I'd moved forward with my life.

In my heart I knew I needed to move on with my life in more ways than one. And the next stage was to also introduce this 'new me' to the outside world and in particular to the opposite sex.

It was time for me to start dating again.

CHAPTER THIRTEEN

DATING AGAIN

The thought of even chatting to a man I didn't know, let alone going out on a date with him, was a terrifying prospect. It was a hurdle I had to get over if I ever wanted to move on with my personal life. Yet the thought still scared me half to death. Not only had I been with Jamie for so long, I now had the added stress of having to tell any new man in my life I only had one leg. I couldn't begin to comprehend how you would bring that up in conversation. Even the thought of saying it out loud to a prospective date terrified me.

Since my gastric bypass, boob job and tummy tuck I was slowly beginning to feel good about myself and I continued to lose the last few pounds of excess weight. These changes in my body were triggering changes in my personality too. I felt like life was flowing back into me. I started wanting to take care of myself not only inside, by eating healthily and keeping up with the exercise programme, but also my appearance on the outside. After years of not even bothering to put on make-up I started to take pride in myself again.

As a treat, and as all my old stuff was decaying in a drawer, I decided to have a makeover. I went into my local MAC make-up store and told them I was feeling dowdy and needed a complete overhaul and a new look. I didn't mention a word about why, as for once I just wanted to be like anyone else. In the end I splashed out more than £300 on make-up. I felt fabulous and looked it too. It sounds like a lot of money, and it is a lot, but for me it was priceless as it represented yet another part of starting to love and take care of myself again.

In my mind I knew, as I would probably leave the Army in the not-too-distant future, I was going to have to think about what to do with my life next. I'd always loved having and giving beauty treatments. Even in Iraq I never skimped on pamper nights. So it seemed natural to me that I should think about pursuing this as a career – although swapping machine guns for nail guns would be quite a lifestyle change! Facing a future potentially without the Army was such a lot for me to take on board, but I knew I had to consider what I wanted to do with the rest of my life.

For me the real light-bulb moment came a few weeks after my MAC makeover when I went to a local beautician near me. I'd always loved having false eyelashes and I was mucking around on Twitter one night when I saw one of the girls from the cast of *TOWIE* had these fantastic long new lashes. So I googled to see where I could have them done and I found a place near me. I booked an appointment and the lovely beautician who applied my lashes asked if I'd like to have my nails done. We got chatting while I had a full manicure – I hadn't had my nails done since I'd ripped them all off in the rubble, so at first I apologised for how unkempt they were.

When she laughed and said: 'Don't be silly, I've seen far worse,' we started gossiping and then I started to tell her what had happened to me. I told her about the day my life had changed, I told her about being buried in the rubble and how my entire world had been torn apart. Then I told her that I had a prosthetic leg. She asked me to show it to her and she was amazed that even though it was quite a basic model, it did have little toes and nails on it. I admitted that the only reason I hated it was because since the blast I hadn't been able to wear any sandals.

Without missing a beat she said: 'Why not? Why don't you just paint your prosthetic toes?'

I then asked: 'Please will you do it for me?' It was the first time I had asked anyone who was a virtual stranger to me to do anything intimate that involved my prosthetic, but I felt so relaxed in there and she was so marvellous that it seemed a natural question to ask. When I left the salon I felt amazing, even though the reality was I'd just had a lick of bright pink varnish on my nails and my eyelashes done. I thought: 'I'd like to help other women feel good about themselves.' So the idea for a future career as a beautician was born.

I spent the next few days researching online what qualifications I would need to train and then set about applying to my local college for them. I had a few thousand pounds saved up to pay for the courses. Within a few months I'd begun training in my spare time. First it was massage, then false eyelashes and then a course on HD brows: basically anything and everything it would take me to become a fully qualified beautician. I must have been one of the college's keenest pupils. I loved going there and roping in all my mates as guinea pigs for treatments. Even my poor mum was getting every treatment under the sun, from waxing to brows! The minute I got one qualification, I was on to getting the next.

As well as my training I was still getting my own beauty treatments done at my local salon. One of the biggest moments was when I decided to go and get my first pair of flat sandals and afterwards, with them still in a shoebox, I went down and had a manicure with my 'good' foot and while it dried, my prosthetic leg had ruby red nails painted on, too. Then I walked out of the salon with my new open-toed shoes on. It was such a small thing, but to be able to go out and have matching feet for the first time in years felt like yet another milestone had been ticked off.

I forged an amazing bond with my beauty therapist, who really helped me to get my confidence back, so much so that she suggested we should go into business together. I thought: 'Why not?' as it seemed like a natural progression for me. We went as far as getting a business plan together and later, we set up a limited company, but I began to get second thoughts as I was worried that I was taking too much on at such an early stage in both my rehabilitation and my beauty training. I couldn't rid myself of the little niggling doubt that maybe this wasn't right for me as I was trying to do too much too soon. After all, I had so many huge decisions to make about my life. I'd overcome so much in such a short time; I'd never run a business before but knew it was going to take a lot of my time and I was just beginning to rebuild not only myself but also my relationship with Milly. The truth is my overriding priority was to be there for her and to make up for all the years of time we lost. After a few weeks of soul-searching I decided I couldn't go on with the business because my family had to come first. I went to the salon to tell my friend and we agreed that as the timing wasn't right for me we would put everything on hold.

Worrying about what I should do with my career and my future did have a small silver lining. The last few pounds of the weight I'd gained when I was ill finally dropped off and I was now back to the size I was in the Army before the blast. People kept saying how well I looked and I knew that the waistbands on the clothes I'd bought as I'd got thinner were getting looser and looser, and they were even beginning to swamp my frame. I knew it was time to measure myself and think about smartening up my appearance.

One night I took the tape measure out and I was astounded when I measured myself and my waist was only 27 inches. I'd finally got down to a size 10 from a 24. It was the final milestone. I was ecstatic and I thought: 'Right, the time has come to get back out there and start socialising properly again with my girlfriends and having a laugh.' I'd missed out on so much of that. I used to love a girlie night out and having a drink and a dance but for years I'd had to shut that entire part of my life and my personality down. It was like I'd pressed pause and now it was time to push the play button again.

Around that time I thought I needed to start thinking seriously about getting a decent wardrobe of clothes again as I'd now reached my target size. I decided, along with some gentle persuasion from Nikki, I couldn't go out on my first proper Saturday night with girls in my baggy tracksuit bottoms and a jumper, so I went on a little shopping spree in my local department store. It was strange looking at some of the little dresses and tops and actually thinking I could wear that and I don't need to hide my body away anymore.

I was still unsure of myself so I took Nikki along to give me some confidence. She was brilliant and really encouraged me to go for it. I played it safe and picked out a lovely black dress which went to my knees and a pair of matching low black heels. I didn't even try them on in the shop – I still felt self-conscious about going into changing rooms in case they were communal and I had to show my body off to other women. Even though I looked great, in my head there was still this little voice telling me I didn't.

When we got back to mine later that afternoon we opened a bottle of wine and spent the next few hours getting ready. I went the whole hog with a fake tan and false eyelashes. When I put on my dress and shoes and stood in front of the mirror I barely recognised myself. For a moment I stood there in silence and Nikki just kept saying: 'Oh, my God, Hannah, you look amazing!' and for the first time since everything that had happened I actually felt it. I just kept running my hands up and down the side of my dress – I couldn't believe how good I looked.

By the time we made our way out that night, my confidence boosted by a glass of white wine, I was buzzing. It was like my first nights out as a teenager. Even though we were only going out to a few of the local bars, to me it was such a big step. It was like being given VIP access to the biggest, best nightclub in the world. I'll never forget walking into the first bar, as for the first time in years I actually strode in with a bit of confidence. I was aware of a few men looking at me as I walked up to the bar to buy us both a drink.

One handsome young guy smiled over at me and then moved beside me in the queue. His chat was really friendly, just the basic stuff like: 'Who was I out with?' and 'Where were we going to be going later on?' I pointed out Nikki and a few of our other friends then he offered to buy us all a drink. I just laughed and said we'd be getting our own. As I walked back from the bar to my friends it dawned on me that speaking to a handsome stranger at a bar wasn't something that had happened to me in a very long time. I had lost so much of my confidence due to the weight gain that as I hadn't liked myself in any way I'd found it incredible that anyone else would. In my head I was still that invisible, fat person. I realised that night that the reality was very different and men were finding me very attractive.

That fleeting conversation with the good-looking stranger changed everything; it changed my entire perception of myself. From then on my confidence just started to grow and grow. Jamie would have Milly alternate weekends and when I had my time on my own, I loved my girly nights out. Blokes were always offering to buy me drinks or they would ask for a number, and while I was polite and maybe had a quick chat and a laugh I didn't take it seriously as it was still a bit of a shock to the system. But as the weeks went by my confidence grew and bolstered by a few white wines I began to relax and let my hair down a bit more. If there was an attractive bloke who offered to buy my mates and me a drink I'd think: 'What the hell! I'll let him.'

The penny had finally dropped that I was attractive again and the person I saw when I looked in the mirror was beginning to change. Gone was the twenty-one stone, one-legged monster and in front of me was a size-10 attractive young woman. It was yet another milestone being reached in my rehabilitation programme and in the accepting of, and learning to love, the person I was.

After I'd been going out on the town for about three months I felt myself getting bolder. By then, I'd been on loads of trips with Blesma, which not only had given me confidence in allowing me to try something new but all the lads who were also there were so 'balls out' about their prosthetics that some of that attitude was rubbing off on me. Many of them wore shorts with their titanium legs – which were often decorated with Union Jacks. They were proud of their prosthetics and why shouldn't they be? After all, we had all lost limbs serving our country. I remember on the first night out on our ski trip one of the lads whipped off his leg and used it as a drinking cup for some of the local lager and everyone toasted our first day on the slopes from it; even the locals joined in. It was such a fun, spontaneous thing to do. It was all about being proud of who you are and what got you to the place you are in, and that's something they taught me in spades. This was one of loads of incidents I'd been part of, so they were all in my mind and firmly in my subconscious.

One night I was standing at the bar and this older guy was giving me some cheesy chat-up lines. It was innocent enough but he was telling me how I was so beautiful I took his breath away. I don't know what came over me, probably my sense of cheekiness fuelled by a couple of drinks, but I spun round and said: 'I've got something that will really take your breath away.' With that, I whipped off my leg and laid it out on the bar. He just burst out laughing and so did I, but he never really batted an eyelid. We ended up having a really good chat about it and he was just so positive and so nice that from that night on it was my modus operandi just to tell people about my amputation and get it out in the open as soon as possible.

As far as men were concerned I'd decided that while I had

lots of fun flirtations I was never going to meet someone serious in a bar in Winchester. I had loads of male friends and lots of admirers, although I never took up any offers, but I was looking for someone I had a special spark with. I wanted a relationship, not a fling. Friends of mine knew a guy they thought I'd like, so one night when we were out in a bar they brought him along. The attraction was instant. He was gorgeous and because he knew friends of mine and he also had Army connections he already knew about my leg. That meant it was no big deal and there was no pressure on me to have to reveal anything to him as he already knew. We'd both done a lot of travelling so we spent the evening with friends, just chatting to them and each other about the places we'd been. Nothing at all romantic happened, even though there was a definite spark. We swapped numbers at the end of the night, which was the first time I'd actually done this with any man since the split with Jamie. While it was a big deal, I was determined to remain fairly casual about it and although I hoped he would contact me, I also thought: 'What the hell? If he doesn't, he doesn't.'

Two days later a text came through, asking me out for dinner at a local restaurant. By the next weekend we were sitting there, just the two of us. The chat flowed all night and we got on so well as we literally had not only some mutual friends in common but shared views on everything, from films to what we liked to eat. It was great fun and we ended the night with a kiss outside the restaurant and then he called me a cab. There was no way it was ever going to be anything more than that as I just wasn't ready, but even though it was an innocent kiss, it was a huge deal for me. I had met a man who I found gorgeous and he felt the same attraction for me.

I was buzzing all the way home in the taxi; I couldn't wait to see him again. The taxi hadn't even pulled up outside my house when the text came through from him saying he'd had a great night and when could he see me again.

That was the start of nearly two months of dating. We had a lot of fun and I was really flattered as although I was feeling so much more confident within myself there was still the tiny voice in my head that said: 'Why is he with someone like me who has only one leg?' I knew, as the relationship was progressing, we would be physically intimate at some point. I had never been with anyone since Jamie, so not only was that a big deal but now I was going to get intimate with a new man while only having one leg. We had gone to the cinema and a few drinks afterwards when he suggested coming back to mine for a nightcap. I knew what that meant and what it might lead to, but it was very much a now or never moment. I really liked him and I knew he felt the same and it was inevitable that our relationship had to go to the next level.

When we got back to mine one thing led to another and it was obvious we were going to take things further and head to the bedroom. My main concern wasn't actually the act of having sex as I could keep my leg on for that, it was the sleeping afterwards, as I have to take my leg off every night to avoid infections. When anyone sleeps they are at their most vulnerable, but I felt even more so with the thought I'd be lying there in bed with a new man with only one leg. I thought: 'Oh, my God, I'm going to feel so exposed!'

I knew it was just another hurdle I was going to have to force myself to overcome and that after I'd done it once I would be able to do it again and it would be easier. I was so nervous but I was going to go through with it. I didn't even turn the lights off – I kept the bedside lamp on. After we made love, I quickly took my leg off in front of him as I sat on the edge of the bed. He made it so natural for me and didn't flinch or say a word. It was like the most natural thing in the world to him. I think deep down he probably was a bit awkward about it all, not because he didn't find me attractive but because he didn't know what to say to me to make me feel better. But then we cuddled up and went to sleep. I could barely shut my eyes as not only was I exhilarated by what had happened, I was so relieved that me taking my leg off hadn't been the massive big deal I'd built it up to be. Again it was another watershed moment to add to the many I'd already had.

We kept dating for the next few months and while it was fun it was beginning to peter out. I felt he was a bit controlling and he started to get a bit jealous of any male friends I had. Retrospectively, I think he knew I wasn't 100 per cent confident in myself or our relationship.

A few months into our relationship he would openly say things like: 'Why do you need to talk to any of those other men as you've got me now?' It started to make me feel a bit claustrophobic and I began to feel a bit isolated as I was spending less time with male friends I'd known for years. One of my close friends whom I'd known since Headley Court actually called me up and said how upset he was because he barely saw me anymore. That was a catalyst. It got me thinking, was this relationship really worth it? Straight away I knew in my heart that the answer was no. I also knew it was never going to go anywhere long term. I had been through so much I just wanted to enjoy myself and looking back, I think I probably wouldn't have been that attracted to him in normal circumstances if I hadn't had my injury.

If I'm being honest with myself I was just flattered he found me attractive, but then I thought: 'I am too strong to turn into one of those women who are grateful to a man just for being with them.' So I made the decision I wasn't going to stick with him just because I couldn't get anyone else and broke off the relationship after about six months.

Although it hadn't lasted, the experience gave me the confidence to start dating properly again, so I do have him to thank for that. I decided I would go the online dating route as it suited me because I was busy; I also had Milly and I knew I wouldn't really meet anyone serious in a bar. I'd come on leaps and bounds with my confidence as I'd jumped the hurdle of being able to tell people about my leg and I knew if I did meet anyone serious and it was going to turn intimate, I had the confidence to cope with that situation as well.

It was also around this time that I decided to put in place the final piece of my body makeover jigsaw and have my second boob job at the beginning of 2013. Before I was blown up, although I was a size 10, I'd always had quite a big bust. And while my first boob job had made a massive difference as my breasts had looked like deflated balloons after my weight dropped off, they were smaller than they were before and I'd also cocked them up with my ski-bob antics. When you have a prosthetic leg it changes your body shape – your bum loses its volume as you no longer use your glutes to walk, instead using your thigh muscles, and I wanted to look in proportion.

So I decided to use £5,500 of my compensation money to go from a C-cup to an E-cup. I found a new surgeon who helped me decide on a high-profile shape this time, which gives a perkier, fuller look. I wasn't nervous before going in as it was a very straightforward procedure. Mum wasn't pleased about me going under the knife again as she thought that this second operation was purely for vanity reasons, but when she knew how strongly I felt about it, she supported me. Some people might find it extraordinary that I made the decision to do that, but when you've lost all your confidence and dignity these things made a massive difference. I didn't have to look at rolls of flab anymore, or loose skin; I looked what I was – a women in her twenties. I think, as well, because I'd had my first bit of intimacy in a relationship I knew there would be more, so I wanted to look and feel the best I could.

Funnily enough, after my operation the surgeon expressed his surprise that one of my implants appeared to be upside down inside me. I didn't have the guts to tell him why! My recovery time was very speedy and I was, and still am, delighted by the results. Finally I was back to being a sexy, attractive young women, I felt. Around this time I invested in a lot of new tops and while I didn't want them all low-cut, I was so proud of the way I was looking and the hard work I had put in to get myself there. I remember it was only weeks after the op when Milly was in bed when I thought: 'What the hell? I'm going to put myself on an Internet dating site.' I grabbed my laptop and did a bit of research. I was looking not just for sex or one-night stands, but actually a place to meet someone for a more meaningful long-term relationship. I put a nice picture on the site and a few paragraphs saying I was a fun and upbeat person looking to have a laugh but for something more than a fling. And also that I was looking for a man who had a similar positive view of life.

I started getting emails through within a few days and within a week I had arranged to go out on a date. It was a disaster from the get-go. We'd arranged to meet at a local bar and he turned up nearly an hour late wearing jewelled cowboy boots. He was wearing two giant earrings and had long bleached blond hair; he was also at least ten years older than he had said he was. I spent the entire hour and a half we were together barely getting a word in edgeways as he felt the need to spend the whole time talking about how he was about to realise his lifelong ambition of owning his own dog kennels. He even went so far as to describe in great detail the type of flooring he was planning to put down. I walked away feeling dejected and thought it couldn't get any worse than that. Little did I know that more than a couple of weeks later it could!

I was determined my first Internet date wasn't going to be my last, so after a few emails with another guy, I decided to go on another date. We met at a local restaurant but when I walked in and saw him sitting there I knew I'd made a big mistake. He was about twenty years older than his profile picture. But I thought: 'Oh well, what the hell? I'll at least sit and have the meal and give him a chance.' I hadn't told him anything at all about my leg as I felt it was far too soon and to look at me you would never know.

We had only just finished our starters and from nowhere he began to tell me about how he was a foot fetishist. I nearly choked on a bread roll. He just kept on and on about how he found feet such a turn-on. This had come from nowhere and in my head I was thinking: 'I've only got one, mate, so you're going to be deeply disappointed!' I excused myself and went to the toilet and never came back. Needless to say I never heard from him again either, thankfully.

I was nearly put off Internet dating completely by this second experience but I'd paid for a three-month subscription to the site so I kept hanging on in there. I went on a few more dates and while the men were really nice and we had a pleasant time together there was really no spark. Then, a few months in, I was matched with someone randomly. They have a feature on the dating site called the roulette wheel, which as you'd expect from the name is a way for people who wouldn't normally be matched by the site getting matched together, like being given a random wild card. A guy called Anthony flashed up and I could see he was attractive from his picture. He obviously felt the same so we started off messaging one another. It was all really basic stuff, but after a few emails over a couple of days he asked me to tell him the most interesting things about me.

I replied: 'My favourite colour's purple and I am the only mum in the British Army to have lost a limb in Iraq.'

He emailed straight back and said: 'Whoa, whoa, whoa, stop right there. What is this about Iraq?'

I replied immediately that the easiest way for me to explain was for him to look at a few of newspaper cuttings that I had about me, which were on my Facebook page. I think I just wanted to get the message out to him really quickly this was who I was, take it or leave it. Anthony emailed straight back and asked me out on a date. I had butterflies in my stomach for I knew this was going to be the start of something big in my life – I just didn't know quite how big at that time.

CHAPTER FOURTEEN

MY MIRACLE

As first dates go, my initial meeting with Anthony in October 2012 was hardly inspiring. We'd been emailing each other for weeks and the banter was great. I knew what he looked like from his photographs, but due to all my previous dud dates I also knew often they bore no resemblance to the person they were supposed to be. When Anthony suggested dinner at a local steak house in Winchester I agreed straight away. I was excited at the thought of meeting him in the flesh and I thought: 'God, I really hope I fancy him.'

He arranged to pick me up and drive me over, which I thought was a really nice, gentlemanly thing to suggest. I was a bag of nerves all day and when the doorbell rang at 6.30pm my hands shook when opened the door. As soon as I saw his bald head and twinkly blue eyes I thought: 'Yeah, he's not too bad. He'll do!' There was no thunderbolt moment, like you see in the movies, but while he didn't totally bowl me over looks-wise, I consoled myself with the fact it was his personality that had attracted me in the first place.

I grabbed my coat and we set off in the car together. There was a really relaxed atmosphere between us; we just got on so well. While there wasn't a massive sexual spark between us that first evening it was fun. Also, as he already knew all about my leg and we'd talked about it before there was no pressure to go over that ground again. For me, that was great as it wasn't the elephant in the room. We spent a fun few hours at the restaurant and when he dropped me off at my house, he went in for a kiss. It didn't last long and while I wasn't left walking on air afterwards, I liked him enough to agree to a second date.

This time he suggested cooking dinner at mine and he rustled up an Italian pasta dish. The chemistry still wasn't there massively for me but it was growing and we did have a right laugh together, so I thought I'd give it a go for a few dates at least.

For our third date I suggested we went to Milton Keynes indoor sky diving, which was completely exhilarating – much more up my street. I'm not sure if it was because we were doing something a bit more daring and we were both out of our comfort zones, but it was the first time I actually felt a sexual spark between us. So, from that point on it snowballed and we embarked on a whirlwind romance and became passionately into each other.

From the start of our relationship Anthony was completely unfazed by my leg. He was the first person I'd come across for whom it wasn't an issue for at all. There was no awkwardness, even when we made love for the first time. Initially, he would lavish me with praise and nice comments about my appearance, which gave my confidence a boost. It was also just a real relief to meet someone who seemed as at ease with my amputation as I myself had become.

In the early days of our romance lots of other things were happening in my life. Just a few weeks after our first date I had my medical board to decide if I would stay in the Army. I had to speak to one female and two male doctors, who wanted to know what I could and couldn't do, what I struggled with at work and if I felt I could still perform in my role in the Army. Once we'd talked everything through, I left the room and sat outside while they deliberated. A short while later they called me back in and told me they were going to give me a medical discharge from the Army. There and then I got my paperwork from the clerk and I was given sixteen months to finish off any medical treatment I needed for my rehabilitation and prosthetics, as well as further retraining as a beautician, which was funded by the Army. Meeting the medical board was a momentous time as it was when I severed my ties with Army life. Although I had a year and a half left, I knew it was over. I walked out with the letter in my hand and immediately when I got home, I phoned my resettlement officer, who helped me with all the additional beauty courses I wanted to do to take it beyond the hobby it had been so far. I felt excited – I was completely ready to start this new chapter in my life. I'd never turn my back on the Army as it had been such a huge part of my life, but I was ready to move on.

I left my Army house and moved in with Anthony in February 2013, renting a sprawling detached property in Northampton. He had a five-year-old son he cared for part-time and with Milly we had a ready-made family. It was a whirlwind romance and I fell deeply in love very quickly, but it felt right as so many new things were opening up for me.

For me, it was also the right time to sever ties with my past life. For years, Jamie and I had never got round to divorcing each other. By now he had also found love again so I rang him and said: 'Do you think it's time that we got divorced?' He immediately laughed and agreed the time had come to finally get the paperwork sorted, as it was just a formality we hadn't got round to doing. As we chatted I remember saying: 'Both our lives are moving on.' I had no regrets as it was absolutely the right thing and to be honest life had just got in the way of us doing it before.

The day my decree absolute came through Jamie got his post first. He texted me to say: 'It's here.' An hour later, mine popped through the letterbox. It wasn't emotional to close such an important chapter in my life, but it did make me think about what an extraordinary husband he'd been. So I texted him: 'I just want to say thank you for everything you did for me and I think we are doing the right thing for Milly.'

Shortly afterwards, he replied: 'Thank you for saying that.' It wasn't sad as we both knew it was coming and I think we both felt quite happy at the way it had gone, but I needed to say that as I'll always be grateful for the kindness and love he gave to me. Without that, I wouldn't be here now, and I decided not to revert back to my maiden name, but to keep the name Campbell as it was the same as Milly's.

As a divorcee, co-habiting with Anthony, life together, at first, was great but a baby was never on the cards. I took a job at Lloyds Pharmacy to help make ends meet and I experienced just one lingering sadness. Four years earlier, during one of my many hospital admissions, I'd asked one of my doctors to tell me if I would ever be able to have anymore children. His answer was quite matter of fact: he said I had a lot of internal scarring from the blast and a high-velocity shrapnel wound had also caused internal damage, grazing my womb and causing a lot of scar tissue. He told me it meant I wouldn't be able to have a baby. At the time I'd felt utter devastation, but I blocked out my feelings or they could have overwhelmed me and at the time I had to focus on getting well. I consoled myself with the fact I was lucky to already have Milly and I forced myself to move on with my life, sad but resigned to the fact I'd never experience motherhood again. I told Anthony early on, as I felt it was right he should know, but as he already had a son, Leo, from a previous relationship he didn't see himself with any more children in his life at that point. So it was never an issue between us.

Under my compensation the abdominal wounds came under the classification of 'high-velocity gunshot wounds', but in fact it was explained to me that shrapnel had entered my body in exactly the same way as a bullet. Even in January 2015 they discovered more of the shrapnel inside my abdomen, which had moved, causing me excruciating pain and an emergency admission to Northampton Hospital.

In addition to those injuries I'd been fitted with a coil for my heavy periods, so when we found out I was pregnant when I was having a routine blood test at the end of August 2013, I was left reeling in shock. Originally I'd been to the doctor as I hadn't been feeling well and when the results came in, the receptionist rang me and said, 'Please can you come in as the doctor needs to discuss with you the results.'

The moment I walked in, he said: 'I think you had better sit down – as you're pregnant.' The room started spinning. I just remember muttering: 'Oh, my God! No, that can't be possible', and I walked out in a daze. I drove home in a state of disbelief, as not only had I suffered those injuries, but I also used the contraceptive coil in order to ease the heavy periods I suffered. I pulled into my drive and then pulled back out again before driving straight back to the surgery to reassure myself I really was having another baby. It just wasn't possible. I never dreamed I'd be a mother again. He had to repeat himself five times as I just didn't believe it. It was only then that it began to sink in, and I felt utter joy and excitement that something so wonderful and miraculous had happened against all the odds.

I drove back home and sat in the drive for a few minutes before going to speak to Anthony, who was at home as he'd recently lost his job. To fill his day he was up a ladder, decorating the bathroom. I just blurted out: 'Anthony, I'm pregnant' and he fell off the ladder in surprise. Luckily he didn't hurt himself but he was shocked, to say the least and he kept gasping in stunned disbelief.

My mothering instinct kicked in the moment I knew of my unborn baby's existence and I loved her. The timing was also extraordinary as it was just three weeks before I was medically discharged from the Army – so it felt as if she was also part of a new start.

When we told Milly she was so excited. I think it was probably the longest nine months of her life, waiting for her little sister.

Once we realised I was pregnant my doctor was immediately concerned that scar tissue from my blast injuries wouldn't stretch, which could prevent my unborn baby from growing properly inside me. So, regretfully I handed in my notice at the pharmacy. As Anthony was also unemployed after losing his job as a marketing consultant, our sole income would be my Army medical pension, but I thought we could make ends meet until he found work.

Every four weeks I went for a scan to make sure things were going OK. Luckily I stayed so tiny during my pregnancy that I never got any bigger than a size 12 all the way through. I watched what I ate once I was over the morning sickness. I had two healthy cravings: raw, cold apples from the fridge and porridge, so luckily my scar tissue didn't become an issue.

I also went to my prosthetics expert to find out the effects of pregnancy on my leg and he said: 'Some people breeze all the way through, others need to have the socket changed if their leg swells up, which can happen in the same way that other prospective mums get swollen ankles. You can also get sores or problems with your hips as your gait changes.' While I didn't suffer from those problems I ended up in and out of hospital, struggling to eat and crippled by unexplained stomach pains, and my illness did put a tremendous strain on us. We'd moved in together quickly, we were having an unexpected baby together, but now, on top of that, an added stress was this devastating illness that left me in and out of the emergency department and having scans, surgery and tests.

Initially, we tried to make things work. Just weeks before Lexi-River was born Anthony proposed to me on Valentine's Day 2014 on ITV's *This Morning* programme, out of the blue. It was a complete surprise, but while I said 'Yes', privately, I already had reservations about whether our relationship would last. However, I resolved to give things a go for the sake of our baby. Even though our relationship was troubled, my impending baby had allowed me to find inner peace and I hoped she'd do that for my relationship as well.

My inner wellbeing wasn't just down to my unborn baby, though. Every year on the anniversary of the blast I'd receive an email from Karl, saying, 'Happy Life Day'. Through our annual email exchanges we shared in the pain of that day and commemorated and celebrated our survival. I can talk to people who have been through similar experiences and tell them what happened but it is never going to be like talking to Karl because he was the only person who was there with me – minutes before it happened and in the aftermath. I've talked to other injured soldiers but no one was there in that instant, moving through what we lived through.

So when I received an email out of the blue on 25 January from him, explaining he'd been feeling low, I wanted to help. He had battled with PTSD in the years since he'd left the Army and Iraq behind, and he felt the time had come to face his demons.

He wrote: 'I've been feeling down. We've spoken about meeting in the past and never done it. What are you doing this weekend?'

Immediately, I replied: 'Here's my address. I'd love to see you.' It was just coincidence that the first day he had free was my thirtieth birthday, on 24 January, but it turned out to be a fantastic birthday present for us both. Karl sat outside for ten minutes, steeling himself to knock on my door. The last time he'd seen me in the flesh was in the hospital bed, days after pulling me from the rubble. He admitted the state I was in when he'd pulled me free had haunted him for years. He'd listened to me screaming, buried alive; he'd used his bare hands to dig me out and he pulled my lifeless body from the rubble.

It wasn't as nerve wracking for me as it was on my territory, so when I opened the front door to see him standing there I just wanted to make him so welcome after all he'd done for me. As he'd written he'd been having a hard time with everything, I'd wondered if it had changed him beyond all recognition. I needn't have worried, though: as soon as I saw him, I just gave him a massive hug and it was like we'd only been apart for a day. It was brilliant to see him again. Time and what had happened seemed to melt away and waves of emotion washed over me at what had happened over the years, but the overwhelming one was of joy to see him again.

While Anthony made us a cup of tea Karl told me: 'I feel such guilt about what happened to you.' I told him that the guilt wasn't his to shoulder. In fact, I think my words were: 'That is the most ridiculous guilt ever – you have nothing to feel guilty for!' I told Karl I wouldn't have met Anthony and I wouldn't have this beautiful baby inside me if the blast hadn't happened.

I firmly explained: 'I am quite at peace with the fact I had to go through such a dark time to get to where I am now. My daughter is a new beginning in my life and I want you to have a new beginning in yours. There's nothing to forgive.' I also wanted him to understand that only one person was to blame in all of this and that was the insurgent who had pressed the button, launching the mortar.

Meeting Karl again was cathartic for both of us. I'd had so many lapses of consciousness that I really wanted to know what had happened to me and I was desperate for him to give me those answers. He managed to fill in a lot of blanks that I had from that day, which meant a huge deal to me and I think from his perspective seeing me looking well, happy and pregnant, meant the world to him. I didn't realise until after our meeting that not knowing exactly what had happened to me during and after the blast still cast a bit of a shadow. Meeting Karl freed me from that as hearing what he remembered and saw helped me fill in the pieces of a jigsaw puzzle that had bothered me for years. We didn't have answers for everything, but it helped such a lot.

After he left, I went out for a birthday dinner with my friends and I started telling them, and then I got emotional as it was just so amazing to have seen him. They said: 'Oh, my God, what an amazing birthday present!' and I have to admit it was one of the best birthday gifts of my life. Since then I've kept in touch with Karl much more closely, messaging on Facebook and speaking. I truly believe that everything does happen for a reason and I feel I had to go through all of that bad stuff to get all of this.

Over the years I've also kept in touch with John Lewis, my friend and the man whose guard duty I took on that fateful day in Iraq, and we've seen each other numerous times since I was injured. John and his wife and kids came to stay with me just a few weeks after I met Karl again. We talked all about the baby and spoke about his kids. We have always got on like a house on fire and nothing has changed. They live in Germany now so it made sense for them all to stay the night. It's like time has never passed when we all meet up, it's always great fun. We don't dwell on what happened in the past as so much has happened to both of us since then; we both have more children and our lives have moved on. We have maintained such a good friendship through everything and now I always think we will. We only talked about that fateful night once, way back at the beginning. Now neither of us ever mentions it. Quite simply, we don't need to and that's now the same with Karl, with whom I know I'll stay in touch for the rest of my life.

By the end of March being pregnant started to take its toll and I developed a serious rash on my stump that threatened to become an open sore. It led my consultant to say: 'Your body has had enough, the safest thing is to do is have a caesarean.'

Against all odds, I gave birth two days later, on 31 March 2014, to a healthy, 5lb 12oz baby girl we named Lexi-River, which means 'saviour and defender'. Anthony and I had put together a CD of music we wanted played in the operating theatre. As they pulled her out of me and she started screaming, my favourite Groove Armada song, 'Just For Tonight', came on. Anthony held her first, until I was able to sit up, then she was put onto my chest. I looked into her blue eyes and the joy I felt was indescribable. 'She's just perfect,' was all I could say as I was crying so much with happiness. Lexi-River screamed the place down and it was an amazing, perfect moment.

I'd never imagined or dared to dream I'd be a mother again. Each time I hold her and look at her piercing blue eyes I feel overwhelming love for this amazing little person I thought would never be here. Anthony specially made up a little pink romper suit on which is written: 'Look, two legs, Mummy!' as an 'in joke' for us, which made me laugh when he got her dressed. Today, I still have to pinch myself to believe I have a beautiful baby. Lexi-River is the most wonderful gift of my life. She was the most amazing, unexpected and miraculous surprise.

After Lexi-River was born our house was full of people for the first two weeks, as everybody wanted to celebrate the fact that she'd arrived safe and sound. As I'd had a caesarean, I was struggling to get around as you use your abdominal muscles more as an amputee, so it was difficult. The slack was taken up by our many visitors, who all wanted to give cuddles and bottle feeds. I honestly couldn't believe my luck during that time after everything that had gone before.

Then, three weeks after Lexi-River was born, I woke up gripped by an agonising pain and I ended up being rushed, yet again, to A&E for a CT scan. I was in surgery within twenty minutes due to a rupture of my stomach and then placed in a high-dependency unit for ten days. All the while Lexi-River was at home alone with my mum, who cared for her with Anthony. They would bring her in twice a day but it was like all my worst fears had been realised: my health was keeping me away from my baby. I felt guilty I wasn't with her and I feared history was about to repeat itself.

Once I was discharged I was so ill, I was unable to carry Lexi-River, so the burden fell on my mother to run the house and care for her as Anthony struggled on his own. My health visitor was amazing too in giving support at that time and I was really able to talk to her about what was going on. Due to the strain of everything my relationship with Anthony broke down. Perhaps it was wrong of me to compare, but while my ex Jamie had risen to the challenge all those years ago, my relationship with Anthony didn't have strong enough foundations and it crumpled like paper. We split up after I came to the realisation: 'I'm going to be better off doing this on my own than I am with you.' By the end he wasn't even my friend, let alone my partner, which was really sad.

For the first time I truly realised and appreciated just how amazing Jamie had been as a partner. His career had suffered as a result of what had happened to me as he spent so much time caring for me that he was passed over for promotion, yet he never made me feel bad or complained; he just got on and did it. He'd never made me feel like a burden with my disability, even through the darkest times when I was mentally ill when I first got home with PTSD, and when he had to care for me before and after my amputation. It was a big shock that Anthony couldn't cope as well when I fell ill. I never wanted to rekindle my relationship with Jamie but I rang him and said: 'I never really appreciated until now just how much you did for me, so thank you.'

We'll never get back together but I admire him and respect him as he's an exceptional person and I'm very proud that he's Milly's dad. Despite the rollercoaster of my relationship and health I was determined it wouldn't affect my bond with Lexi-River and I wouldn't miss out – and I haven't. She's an absolute joy and I have Anthony to thank for bringing her into my life.

Nikki was also there, along with Mum, to help me through the worst of the split. She took a week off from the Army from her role as Lance Sergeant in the Household Cavalry in London to stay with me and she helped me when I was still recovering and feeling exhausted. She'd say: 'You go to bed and I'll do the first night feed so you'll have a longer sleep, and then you can do the second night feed and I'll have a lay-in in the morning.' She really helped me when I needed it. She's still there on the other end of the phone for me now to give her advice about dating or baby issues. It's the strongest friendship I made in the Military without a doubt, as it seems at every milestone or hurdle, Nikki has been there. Nikki leaves the Army in 2016 to focus on a new chapter in her life. She now has two children: Chloe, who is ten years old, and a son Stuart, who is now eight. She plans to move to

Northampton, so it will be just like old times, as neighbours popping in and out of each other's houses now that we are both single mums.

Even in my darkest hours after the split I felt I had found a new inner confidence and a new sense of peace. Finally, I was taking control of my own life. I was putting all my past demons to bed and thinking now of the future and what I had to do to ensure it was going to be a bright one.

CHAPTER FIFTEEN

FACING THE PAST AND MOVING ON

There has always been a little niggle at the back of my mind that the one thing I had never really faced up to properly was my old self. Well, the celebrity picture of my old self, to be precise. After I did the shoot with Bryan Adams all those years ago I didn't give it much more thought because, as I said earlier, when I'd seen the pictures I'd hated myself in them. Initially, when they went on show at London's National Portrait Gallery in 2013, I was invited to go and see them but I just couldn't face it.

I'd found out I was pregnant with Lexi-River, so I had countless emotions running through me and the thought of standing there, staring at a picture of myself at the bleakest time in my life, looking and feeling my worst, was the last thing I wanted to do. I've barely looked at the images since then; the only use I have now for the hardback book they are in is as either a door-stop or as something to support Lexi-River's feet when she plays in her baby bouncer at home as she's still too small for her toes to reach the ground. So, it came as a surprise when my mum found out from one of her friends that the exhibition, *Wounded: The Legacy of War*, was running again in London at Somerset House in November 2014. Mum spent a few days deciding whether or not to tell me and the thought did cross her mind just to let it go, as I wouldn't have been any the wiser. In the end, she thought it was something I should know as I feature in it. When she told me, during one of our phone calls, my gut reaction was: 'Oh God, not again!'

While I'm still glad I posed for Bryan Adams, I was only at the start of my recovery, so it was just a snapshot of a moment in time – and not a good one at that. It's because of the timing in my life that I hate the pictures and the odd few times I have looked at them in the book I have had to quickly close it. It's hard to look at myself when I know at that time, in May 2011, I was just horribly sad and my life was in a very dark, weird and vulnerable place. I was simply dragging myself along and I wasn't living but only just surviving. So it was as if once more the pictures and the spectre of my past self had come back to haunt me.

I was wound up at first, as a part of me knew I should go and see it, but a bigger part of me didn't want to. Because I had moved on so much with my life I had to ask myself seriously: 'Why am I so bothered about seeing the images again?' I think I was always fearful, up until that point, of looking at them in case it took me back to a place where I didn't want to go. That meant, unlike everything else in my life, I didn't hit it on the head; I avoided it. It was an ostrich-in-the-sand approach, which just isn't me at all.

The thought kept niggling away for a few weeks before I

thought again to myself: 'Right, this is ridiculous! I'm going to go and see myself and put this ghost to rest.' I told no one I was going except my mum; I was determined my girls would be there with Mum and me as well. It would give me a chance to remind Milly how far we've come and I wouldn't dream of going there without Lexi-River too. The first chance I had time to go and see the exhibition was the start of January 2015 so it seemed a fitting way to kick off the New Year. Making peace with the images of your former self certainly beats giving up chocolate or a glass of wine on the New Year's resolutions list!

The four of us took the train from Northampton to London and got ourselves to Somerset House. As our black cab pulled up, I felt surprisingly calm about it. We'd chosen to go early on a weekday morning as I was convinced it would be quieter and I wanted to make sure we were the only ones around. The exhibition was in one of the back wings of the museum so it was tucked away. What I wasn't prepared for was how big some of the images were. When I walked into the stark white room I caught my breath and grabbed Milly's hand, more to support me than her. My mum held Lexi-River in her arms and the four of us went in.

I'd spoken to Milly about it on the train down and told her: 'Mummy's picture is hanging in a famous gallery in London but it won't look like Mummy now, it's Mummy from before.' She'd already seen the pictures when I got the book several years ago and she still has some memories of me being like that, but she takes it all in her stride – it's just Mummy to her so it all seems very normal. Inside, it was like a who's who of people I knew hanging on the wall, three feet high: triple amputee Mark Ormrod, a Royal Marine Commando, was there; Sergeant Rick Clement, who had lost both of his legs above the knee after an explosion in Afghanistan, and a second Royal Marine Commando, Joe Townsend. My heart was racing when I saw them all in the same room together. I felt a few tears stinging as I could see a lot of pain in some of their eyes. I know how they must have been feeling as I have had those feelings, too. Yet each photo relayed an overwhelming sense that despite the broken bodies and wounds there was also courage, defiance and humour.

Walking through into a second room, it then hit me. On the wall, on the left-hand side, nearly three feet high and in full technicolour was me. I was standing side on, wearing my camouflage uniform, with my first titanium leg on show. Staring at the photograph led my heart to flip over and my pulse to race: finally, after everything, I was looking back at myself. Mum looked quite emotional, but she's always been stoic and for a few minutes we stood before the image in silence. When I looked into the eyes of the woman in the picture, while my stance at first glance looks proud, all I could see was that I'd become a shadow of the young women I used to be, filled with misery. Recognising this also led to a kind of mental release for it's something that isn't there anymore. I turned to Mum and simply stated: 'That isn't me.'

With that, a feeling of relief flooded over me. Here I was, facing myself, and a place in the past I have fought so hard to leave, but I've also been so scared to look back at. Finding the courage to look back meant I now knew categorically that I had left it behind. Gone is the old Hannah in the picture, banished to the past where she belongs. I felt euphoric and wished I'd done it all those years before, but everything takes time and for me the right time was now.

A few other visitors to the exhibition had filtered into the room by now so we weren't alone. As people looked at the images one woman stood beside me and said to a male friend who was with her: 'God, look at that poor woman! She's been through so much. I wonder where on earth she is now?' I wish I'd been braver but I didn't say a word, and thank goodness Milly didn't hear her or she wouldn't have been able to stop herself from piping up: 'It's Mummy!' as she's so proud of me.

As I turned to walk away, I gave her a smile. She smiled back completely unaware I was, in fact, the woman in the picture. That cemented in my mind that I am now completely unrecognisable as the Hannah hanging on the wall. Seeing the photograph again in all its glory was just another stepping stone in the journey forward with my life. Milly asked me: 'Are you OK, Mummy?'

I hugged her and said 'yes' and then she asked to go to the café for a drink and something to eat. Just like that we all turned and walked out of the room. It was as if we'd walked away from that chapter of my life into a new one and I couldn't have been happier to close the door firmly shut. As I strolled out into the sunshine, with Lexi-River in her pushchair, Milly's hand in mine, and my mum by my side, I felt euphoric and I didn't look back. Everyone I loved was there in that split second right beside me and I felt strong and complete. I knew the demons were going forever and I was emerging again: my girls and me could do anything.

The three of us have become so close since Anthony and I split up. Once I'd got over the initial stages of being scared of being on my own I began to love life with just the girls. Through Lexi-River I had started to meet other young mums in the area at baby massage; I'd also made a lot of friends now Milly was at school. My health visitor was brilliant as well – she was coming out to the house regularly and getting me involved in lots of stuff for the kids, like playgroups. I was rebuilding my life without Anthony and determined to get out and about, adjusting to being a single mum.

Don't get me wrong, it wasn't easy, and anyone who says being a single mum is has never walked in one's shoes. You have to do everything 24/7. And if Lexi-River cries in the night, unlike other mums, I'm not able just to jump out of bed: I have to take a few extra seconds to put my leg on and then go to her. It was harder, but I got on with it. I had to – there wasn't any other choice.

As Lexi-River grew older, week by week things started to get easier. We got into a great routine and Milly, Lexi-River and I were like a tight-knit little three-man unit, ready for anything. I felt whatever life threw at us, what the hell, we pulled together and we handled it. In some ways it was a relief to be on my own for I just had to look after my daughters and myself. I just counted my lucky stars that I had such great friends and family, who I could rely on at even the hardest of times. The help from Milly has been invaluable – she has always been totally brilliant and a proper big sister to Lexi-River. She just has to walk into a room and Lexi-River has the biggest smile for her. Now Lexi-River has grown up a bit, Milly is able to play with her properly and when she was a newborn, Milly was always running and fetching things for me, like nappies and baby wipes. I don't think I would have managed without her. Our relationship is so strong and we share a unique bond.

After all we've been through, there is something very special about my relationship with Milly. Being aware of the influence I have in shaping her life has made me refuse to be a miserable person, consumed with bitterness about my injury. The truth is, that as an amputee if I said to people: 'I can't do that, I've only got one leg,' they would accept it. But I didn't want to be that person to my daughter: I didn't want to be defeatist; I wanted to do better.

Now she's coming up for eleven years old, I think Milly has started to realise how important she's been in getting me to where I am today. I know today, without a shadow of doubt, that my daughter is proud of me. She tells her friends at school about me and my former life in the Army, and that I'm a special mum. Maybe she would have been proud of me even if I hadn't done wild things like skiing or running a marathon, who knows? Today I feel that we have a stronger bond than most mums and daughters, though. I suppose not every mum would go out of their way to do extreme things to make their daughter proud of them but not every mum can look at their daughter and know that she gave her the strength to go on.

Of course, I also love Lexi-River to bits as she is my miracle baby. I've enjoyed her as a baby so, so much. She is such a happy little girl. The miracle of her even being here has given me the chance to enjoy all the things I missed out on with Milly as my life was blighted by injury. Going to the park or to a play group wasn't as easy with Milly as I was in the Army; I had to put my job first as that's what I'd signed up to. Then after that I couldn't go due to my injuries. This time around, with Lexi-River, this isn't an issue and I can relax and enjoy watching her grow up. When she gets older she will never have known me as anything other than an amputee, so to her having a mummy with one leg will be the most natural thing in the world. It is natural now to Milly, but as she knew me before and was there throughout all the devastating aftermath of my injuries we've had to work through the tough times together. With Lexi-River there's none of that.

In addition, I haven't been treated for PTSD for many years now. While there's always a chance it could return later in life, I've got the coping strategies in place to be able to deal with it, if it ever resurfaced. There are amazing charities like Combat Stress, who are doing so much, and they have helped many of my friends.

One other thing that took my mind off the split from Anthony was that we had to move house. We had a beautiful, massive seven-bedroom place but because it was now only the three of us, we had to downsize – it seemed silly to have such a big place with us rattling around in it. We spent months searching for somewhere and then this beautiful period property in Northampton came up. The minute we walked in the front door to view it, I knew I'd found our home. We got the keys a few weeks later and we've been there ever since. It's got such a happy atmosphere. I've got all our family pictures up in a giant collage in the kitchen. Milly and Lexi-River's toys are scattered everywhere but that's how it should be; the house is filled with love and laughter. When I look back at our old place it feels like it was such a burden and, while it was a beautiful house, it didn't have a soul. Anthony, who lives close by, regularly takes Lexi-River twice a week, which gives him bonding time with our beautiful daughter.

I also had something else in my diary to look forward to just after we moved: I was going to realise an ambition of mine to be on ITV's *Loose Women*. I loved the show and used to watch it all the time from the comfort of my sofa, so when one of the producers approached me to appear in their Armed Forces special with Lexi-River, to talk about my life in the Army and how far I'd come, and of course how my life had now moved on, I agreed straight away. But the minute I put the phone down on them I thought: 'Oh my God, I'm nervous! What have I done?'

The show was only weeks away and I was determined to look and feel my best, so, I bought a new dress and got my hair and nails all done ready for the show. I felt so privileged to be asked to take part and share my story about life in the Army, being a mum on the frontline, and recovering from terrible injuries doing my job. I also wanted to take Milly with me so she would have the amazing experience of being with me in a TV studio, so I arranged for her to have the day off from school and the show booked a taxi to take us all the way from Northampton to the TV studios, which are on London's Southbank. Even the journey down was exciting, especially for Milly. She felt so special sitting in the back of this posh taxi; it was great fun.

We got a special room behind the scenes and Milly was so excited because it had a little fridge in it, filled with drinks and snacks she could help herself to. I had my make-up done by two professional stylists. I was nervous that I was going to slip up and say something silly as it was live TV, but having Lexi-River with me made it easier and my main concern was that she was going to bawl her eyes out right there in the middle of *Loose Women*. But I needn't have worried – she was the perfect baby. I think my interview went well and it was great being able to talk about what life is like for women in the Army and to show the world that even though you are an amputee, you can still have a life; you can have a family and both can be pretty amazing. I wanted to try and put over the positive message that just because I had been through an horrific time, it didn't necessarily mean that I was going to curl up and die in a corner. I hoped that maybe I would help someone else sitting at home who may have suffered something life-changing like myself to say: 'Right, if Hannah Campbell can get on with things then so can I!'

I also got to meet a few of the celebrities who were guest presenters on the show that day: Myleene Klass and Janet Street-Porter, who were fantastic, and everyone was making a fuss of Milly and Lexi-River, who loved it! The whole thing was a complete whirlwind but I'm just so glad I went through with the experience as it was so positive. While I pushed myself to do it, as it was very much out of my comfort zone, I felt I came across well and promoted a very positive image not only of the Army but also of disability.

The only slight blot on the landscape for me throughout the whole of this time has been my chronic stomach problem. Since autumn 2014, when the wheels came off my recovery, I've been repeatedly admitted to hospital with severe abdominal pain. Daily pain with your stomach is so debilitating and the doctors took a while to get a proper diagnosis of my condition, so I was starting to fear that something was seriously wrong with me. I began to get quite bad anxiety attacks with it as well as I became terrified I was dying and that I would leave my girls without a mum. While I wasn't able to control whatever was causing the pain, I was able to control my mind and in turn my reaction to it, thanks to the counselling I'd received. My rationale was that if everyone was afraid of what was around the corner and the unknown then no one would ever get out of bed in the morning!

After a series of medical investigations over the course of the next six months, it was discovered that I had a couple of perforated ulcers and suspected chronic pancreatitis. More shrapnel was found in my abdomen in December 2014 and this has caused some additional problems. With such tiny fragments, doctors have to weigh up the risks of abdominal surgery – and often tiny pieces can cause no harm and can be difficult to remove. I have a pea-sized lump of shrapnel in my left bum cheek, which causes me no trouble at all – and getting people to guess what it could be is one of my party tricks as well as thumping out my prosthetic leg on bar tops! But unfortunately, I have had to have several bouts of surgery again, which after everything I've been through came as quite a blow. As soon as they told me what the name of my illness was I thought: 'Well, at least I know what's wrong and now I'm going to deal with it.' The doctors also told me that during one of my scans I had endometriosis, which causes infertility and makes Lexi-River's conception even more of a miracle.

I see these health issues as a temporary blip and for the first time in a very long while, I finally feel like now I have found my place: I am just so happy and contented. When I look in the mirror I actually like myself again. I've looked good for a while, or so my friends have all told me! Now I actually feel it and believe them. Some people may think that undergoing the amount of cosmetic surgery I've had is extreme but the whole experience of what I've been through *is* extreme. It's hard to love yourself when you're covered in stitches from countless operations to try and save your sight or your face, or help with your leg. To be honest, at times it feels like the war I've been fighting is with my own body. Even now, because of the gastric bypass I have to watch what I eat and it's really hard. I go to the gym twice a week and I take multivitamins daily to ensure I've got all the nutrients I need and I've maintained my weight at 9 stone.

In total, I've spent around just over £52,000 of my compensation money on cosmetic surgery and other beauty treatments. I knew I was never going to be perfect but then I wasn't looking for perfection, which is something I think those people who become addicted to plastic surgery are looking for. I knew that would never be possible as I only have one leg and countless shrapnel and operation scars, so straight away, these are what some might regard as 'imperfections' that with the best will in the world cannot be fixed, and I accept that. Personally, I see them as a history of my journey. But I also wanted to face the world as a woman in her twenties. While I knew any surgery would leave further scarring, I wanted to improve as best I could what I felt had been damaged by the blast. Removing my excess skin, getting back the breasts that I had before, and perking my face up with a bit of Botox not only because my eye had dropped but because I felt the whole experience had aged me considerably, all helped me find myself again. There's an Army saying: 'You look like you've have a paper round in Baghdad' – and that's how I felt about my appearance. The stress of it all had taken its toll on both my body and my looks.

Without my injuries I would never have been someone who would have gone in for plastic surgery. Maybe I would have had my boobs done but that's only a maybe! The compensation money is there to compensate you for everything you have suffered. My body and face took the worst of the hit, so that's why I used some of the cash to get back some of what I lost. I have also learned that while I have regained some of who I was before, I've also become a new person. What has happened has changed me and I'd say I've became a far more compassionate person than I was before, and I think that everything I've been through has ultimately made me a better person too.

For the past few years, as I have grown in confidence and acceptance of myself, I have been asked by other injured service people for my advice and to tell my story of what I've been through. I'm always delighted to help and always have the time to spare.

Another female soldier, who was injured in a freak accident, asked for my advice when she had to make the tough decision as to whether to elect for amputation after years of surgery on her leg. Her situation was almost identical to the one I found myself in, although she'd persevered for more years than me, trying to save her limb. Our meeting was like a role reversal of the time I met Captain Kate Philp. She asked me almost exactly the same questions, including: 'How do you go for a wee in the middle of the night?' and 'Do you wear heels?' – which made me laugh. It allowed me to reflect on how far I've come in a relatively short space of time. At that point I was in a really good place with my prosthetics and I said: 'Elective amputation was the best thing I did. That's not to say it will be the best thing for you, as that decision can only be made by you alone. All I can say is for me, the choice of being in a wheelchair or having an active life was a no-brainer.' The last time I saw her she had gone ahead and had her leg amputated. Like me, she never looked back. She's inspirational and I'm still in touch with her now.

Helping her to set the wheels in motion to rebuild her life got me thinking about my own future. I have had a lot of help in being rebuilt from the inside out from lots of different people since I was injured. This includes everything from building confidence to how to dress when you have a prosthetic leg.

I've been lucky to have received help from the Army through Headley Court and lots of other organisations like Blesma, from my surgeon Professor Sir Keith Porter, personal trainers who've helped me to get fit and even personal stylists. So what I really want to do now is to start a charity that helps other people who have also endured life-changing injuries. I want to provide a support network that helps people rebuild themselves, find their inner confidence again and face life. The onus will be on helping them to ultimately help themselves and learn how to carry on with their lives after really serious injuries. I've had so much help along the way from other people and I feel I have a lot to give myself; also, I want to work on getting a strong team of people together to help as well.

In addition to the Army, the services charity Blesma and the time I have spent with them since first having my leg amputated has been fundamental in my rehabilitation process. From taking me skiing to motor-biking to even running the marathon, they've helped me achieve the impossible. I want to do similarly for not only former service personnel, but also civilians who don't get access to something like this despite their injuries; I want to provide a charity which helps people in the Military but is also open to all.

I also hope to inspire others, particularly my children. And my newfound confidence led me to undertake my first skydive in 2015. I turned up at a local centre with my friend Dale Leach who is also a former soldier and a left-leg-above-knee amputee who I'd met in Headley Court. I was scared half to death but not so worried as the staff when I insisted I wanted to wear my prosthetic leg! They were worried that the rush of wind would send it whizzing off through the air. But nothing would make me take it off.

'I won't jump unless I'm allowed to wear it,' I said, explaining that I see my leg as my independence. They agreed, although I had to sign a waiver, and so up we went in a plane. As the expert counted down for the tandem jump, I thought, 'God, what have I done?' But the next thing we were in the air and it was the most exhilarating experience I've ever had. And thankfully my Headley Court prosthetic went the distance.

Shortly after, in May 2015, I made a trip back to the Queen Elizabeth Hospital in Birmingham to see Professor Sir Keith Porter. For the first time I felt well enough and in a good enough place in my life to properly thank him for what he and his team have done for me. I wrote a letter to him and shortly after I was thrilled when he agreed to meet. As soon as I saw him, in a private room at the hospital, I just walked up to him and gave him the biggest hug, before saying, 'Thank you for chopping my leg off!'. He was at pains to tell me he was just one part of a much bigger team, but I was thrilled that he remembered me and I told him that without him my life would be nothing like it is today and I'll always be grateful to him.

One of the things which strikes a chord with me and that I find sad is that troops are now heading back to Iraq in 2015; it makes me fear others may be injured there again, just like I was. When I heard it was going to happen I was filled with abject horror. It made me wonder why on earth we were going back there as it makes a mockery of all the work we did. Also, how many other men and women are going to be injured on the frontline in horrific ways and come home just like me? On learning this, my mind immediately went back to the day I was injured and the hell I endured, suffocating to near-death under the rubble of a building. What on earth was it all for? Why the hell have I, and hundreds of other servicemen and women and their families, gone through what we did to then go back and potentially start it all up again? It's a farce that we have withdrawn from Afghanistan and the conflict zone there only to go back into another. I think that the cost of withdrawing has probably been more than if we'd just stayed in Iraq in the first place. It seems such a bizarre political dance that we've gone through only to end up straight back at square one again. I feel cheated and angered by it. I don't know anyone who is going back and while I've kept in touch with a few close friends who are still serving, I have drifted away from many others. It seems natural as my life has moved on, and so has theirs. I will never forget the times and experiences we've all shared, though, and I'm lucky to count a few, including Nikki, as firm friends for life. Her journey is also coming full circle as she leaves the Army in 2015 and is buying a house on the next street over from me, so it will be just like the old days.

The Chilcot Inquiry is also supposed to be released later in 2015 and I await its findings with interest. As a former soldier, when you speak to civilians about Iraq there's often contempt and that's really difficult to hear, especially when you've paid a price with your health for so long. I always explain as a soldier we are paid to do a job and I wasn't paid to think about the politics behind it. That said, it's not easy to hear people say: 'You didn't achieve anything by being out there' – particularly when you are missing a limb. I'm immensely proud of having served in the Army and every soldier I knew was proud to have served. That said, I feel in order to get on with my life I've had to cut the cord. It's very easy not to, but if you don't then it's almost impossible to adapt to life outside as a civilian.

Someone asked me what my new focus is in life and that's an easy question to answer: it's my girls. I was also recently asked, 'If you could pass on one thing to them what would it be?' My answer is 'resilience'. Life does throw you a few curve balls and you need to be able to deal with them. I want my girls to be strong, independent woman (as Beyoncé would say!) but if you add resilience to the mix, well that's quite a potent combination. They'll be able to cope with whatever life throws their way.

My amputation means I have a daily reminder of what I went through and my time in service for the rest of my life, but I can see a life for myself and it's going to be a great one. So now, on 18 June, the day I was blown up in Iraq in 2007, when the email from Karl Croft drops into my inbox, simply saying, 'Happy Life Day', I know unequivocally that my life won't just be happy – it is going to be FANTASTIC!

CHARITIES AND ORGANISATIONS

Blesma: www.blesma.org
Queen Elizabeth Hospital Birmingham Charity:
  www.qehb.org
Help For Heroes: www.helpforheroes.org.uk
Bike Tours For The Wounded:
  www.biketoursforthewounded.co.uk
Press People: www.presspeople.co.uk
Combat Stress: www.combatstress.org.uk